Enc

"Held together by the scar tissue of time, I read in wonder as our hero strings together pearls of wisdom from a life of disequilibrium—but with an even greater ability to perpetually resurrect herself into The Look Up Girl."
—John D. Capobianco, D.O., F.A.A.O.

"Shane's story and message are equally stunning; her journey is both heartbreaking and breathtaking as she moves through her life with the spirit of a flower child, only to have her heart, peace, and safety repeatedly challenged and compromised. With fierce resilience and a contagious sense of optimism, Shane shares not only a bumpy ride with us but also the beautiful pieces along a checkered path that offer readers valuable tips for a purposeful life. Get ready for a wild ride and relax, so you don't get whiplash."
—Jill Armijo, PTA, CHC, author,
speaker, and self-care coach

"Wow, I could not put this book down! Shane is a talented writer and a beacon of light to all who have faced adversity and struggled to find their way. She gives each of us hope and inspiration that through faith, determination, and a positive attitude, there is a rainbow at the end of the storm. Wonderful book!"
—Barbara Kane, lifelong educator, two-time recipient
of the New Jersey Governor's Award, and proud friend of
Shane brought together by the late Tom Kane

Broken Little Believer

Finding Purpose in All the Pretty Painful Pieces

SHANE SVOREC

Published by Author Academy Elite
PO Box 43, Powell, OH 43065
www.AuthorAcademyElite.com

Identifiers:
LCCN: 2021909180
ISBN: 978-1-64746-807-1 (paperback)
ISBN: 978-1-64746-808-8 (hardback)
ISBN: 978-1-64746-809-5 (ebook)

Available in paperback, hardback, e-book, and audiobook

All Scripture quotations, unless otherwise indicated, are taken from the Holy Bible, New International Version®, NIV®. Copyright © 1973, 1978, 1984, 2011 by Biblica, Inc.™ Used by permission. All rights reserved worldwide.

Any Internet addresses (websites, blogs, etc.) and telephone numbers printed in this book are offered as a resource. They are not intended in any way to be or imply an endorsement by Author Academy Elite, nor does Author Academy Elite vouch for the content of these sites and numbers for the life of this book.

Some names and identifying details have been changed to protect the privacy of individuals.

Dedication

I dedicate this book to the special people who were purposefully placed along my path and who chose to believe in me, support me, root for me, and love me. To my many powerful angels who walk beside me, offering comfort and loving reassurance by way of "no coincidence" signs, they remind me that I am not alone, and love never dies.

To my husband who tirelessly pushed me to write this book, even when I didn't believe it deserved my time or attention, and to my beautiful children who always make me feel like the greatest mom in the world, even at times when I felt like the worst, I owe all of my gratitude. You've loved and accepted me unconditionally and graciously shared me with others who, at times, got the better version of me.

To Lainey, Destiny, and Jack: I wrote this book for you so that you would know that there isn't anything you can't overcome. There is no greater joy, privilege, or accomplishment that I am prouder of than being your mom.

Table of Contents

Section 1
Where the Road Begins

Section 2

Destination Unknown

Section 3

Lost and Disoriented

Section 4
The Long Way Back

Foreword

The very first thing that I noticed about Shane was her incredible way with words. At a women's retreat, we were sitting at separate tables when she shared some reflections on a talk, and I thought, *Wow! What beautiful words and connections she made and said so eloquently. Who is she?* After nervously taking the podium and sharing my story later that day, I was touched that Shane looked for me afterward. She shared some of her magical words and thoughts with me—words that affected and encouraged me, along with a genuine hug that made me want to never let go.

From that first encounter, I have been blessed to become a best friend of Shane's and have learned so much about her incredible life. From beginnings that you would never guess to shocking events, heart-warming stories, and encounters with angels, it's hard to imagine that so much could be packed into one life. And just when you think you know it all, Shane has another unforgettable story to share.

So now, years later, it is no surprise to me that Shane has written a book filled with her life stories to help others find purpose in their own. She shows how it's possible to not only put the pieces of a "broken" life back together, but reassemble them better than before. Shane has a rare ability to understand what others feel and need, sometimes without a word spoken. Whether it's an in-person encounter, a social media post, a thoughtful note, or a piece of writing shared on The Look Up Girl page she created, you can count on Shane to find beauty, purpose, and connections in even the simplest everyday things.

Shane not only speaks (and writes) a good game, she puts her money where her mouth is. She fosters children (including finding those who have aged out of the system and inviting them to holiday dinners), rescues animals, serves on her town's Board of Education and other committees, is active in her church, and is the first to volunteer when someone needs help.

Perhaps many of Shane's stories originate from her being the one to notice and act when something doesn't seem right. When Shane asks if everything is all right or if you are ok, there is an aura about her that just makes one want to open up and talk with her. She listens to what you share and then beautifully weaves an answer, a hope, a prayer, a spark, a connection, a string of thoughtfully chosen words that perfectly fit what you need at that moment. The world certainly could use more Shanes!

So, whether you're going through some difficulties in life, feel lost or disconnected in some way, or just looking for some inspiration, I encourage you to read Broken Little Believer. In it, you're sure to find at least one story that will resonate in some way. You will learn that all things are possible, and no hurdle is too high if you approach it with hope, faith, and positivity.

There are many twists and turns in this book, things you won't see coming—remarkable adventures and tales of love and light that make it impossible to put the book down once you start reading it! Shane will take you on an unforgettable journey that will make you laugh and cry and will touch your heart. And you'll listen to some great music along the way too!

After reading Broken Little Believer, you realize that we never really know what someone is dealing with or has gone through in the past. You see why it is essential to treat everyone you encounter with kindness and leave them feeling like someone special. Shane is the embodiment of that. She is the real deal...SO VERY REAL, and I'm sure after reading her book, you will love her *almost* as much as I do.

Mary Ann Hollar

Preface

*"Other people are going to find healing in your wounds.
Your greatest life messages and your most effective
ministry will come out of your deepest hurts."*[1]
Rick Warren

I have lived my life believing these words and wrote this book in hopes that others might find comfort, hope, or inspiration in mine. Pain is never in vain if we find purpose in it, and how we use our pain determines if we become bitter or better.

Life is messy, unpredictable, and things are not always as they seem, but the power of connection—whether it be to another person, faith, nature, mind, body, or spirit, is where truth resides and hope is born. One of the greatest gifts we can give to another is the reassurance that we are not alone. Just knowing that someone believes in us, cares, or wants to be present, makes all the difference in someone's life.

We all face challenges and endure hardships. Whether anxious or uncertain over world events, personal circumstances, or things we go through, we decide whether we want to use our experiences for good and allow them to serve as an example or as an excuse.

I share my "pieces," hoping that one or two of them might help someone else.

I wrote this book to remind my children and those I love that it's in the not-so-perfect parts that we find truth and others find healing.

To you, the reader, know you are loved and not alone. Hold on to hope and keep believing in a brighter, better tomorrow. Our pieces connect us all—the pretty and the painful ones.

When you're feeling down, LOOK UP!

Xoxo
Shane

Acknowledgments

I would like to thank the following people:

Barbara Kane – Thank you for being one of my Beta-readers, an excited endorser, special friend, and the love of the late Tom Kane, my hero.

Mary Ann Hollar – Thank you for being one of my Beta-readers, my walk and talk it out friend, supportive sister, and confidant.

John Capobianco – Thank you for being one of my Beta-readers and co-editor, a longtime friend and spirit mate.

Jill Armijo – Thank you my meant-to-be-friend and sister in faith, for your mad editing skills.

Alaina Elizabeth – Thanks to the owner of Alaina Elizabeth Photography, a photographer extraordinaire who captures incredible moments and stunning author headshots.

Marsha, Mony, and Mary Ann (My 3Ms) – Thanks for being the "tape" that held me together during some tough times.

@difrats – Thanks to a fabulous graphic and cover design genius.

Jesse Marquez and Jennifer Johnson – Thanks to my long-time friends and beautiful supporters. Thank you for your contributions to this book, but most importantly, for your ongoing friendships.

Rich, Lainey, Destiny, & Jack – I love you! Thanks to my beautiful family for loving, understanding, and always supporting me.

My mom and brother –Thank you both for keeping me grateful for every moment—the good, bad, and the crazy ones. I wouldn't be who I am if it wasn't for you and the roads we traveled. I love you.

I thank all my family and friends, both past and present, for the love you've shown me, the lessons you've taught me, and the light you've shared. I love each connection, relationship, and encounter with you, and I am grateful and better for every one of them.

Love,
Shane

Reader's Check In Here Before the Road Trip

Congratulations! You are about to embark on a journey. Before starting off, you must first acknowledge and accept the following:

- You are voluntarily going on a road trip. Your participation along the way will enhance your riding experience.

- Any preexisting conditions or preconceived notions should be documented on the "Baggage to Be Checked" form.

- There are no reserved or first-class assignments. Seating is open, and all sections offer unobstructed views.

- You are responsible for your baggage; be sure to tag all of your personal belongings and monitor them carefully.

- All tolls, fuel, parking, and travel expenses will be paid for by the driver. Sit back and enjoy the ride!

- There will be unexpected stops and delays along the way. Please be patient and understanding.

- This road trip will not only take you to different places but will open your eyes to new experiences and introduce you to many people.

Last but not least, please be advised that the driver controls the music and has prepared a playlist.

*Follow along with the Spotify playlist titled *Broken Little Believer* and be sure to press play when and where indicated.

Attention Traveling Reader

*Check Baggage, Document Pre-existing Conditions, Preconceived Notions, and Existing Beliefs Here:

Baggage to Be Checked:	Baggage Weight: Scale (1-10) 10 being the heaviest
Despair	
Anger and Frustration	
Grief or Loss	
Loneliness	
Unfulfillment	
Trauma or Illness	
Negativity	
Abuse or Neglect	
Dysfunctional or Unhealthy Relationships	
Inability to forgive yourself or others	
Resentment	
Other	

Now, consider the following questions:

- What has lead you to overcome obstacles?
- What motivates you to get up repeatedly?
- Why do you keep fighting?
- Where do you find hope?

- How do you remain positive when surrounded by negativity?

- Where do you find encouragement?

Is personal satisfaction determined by how or where a person grows up? Is it the environment in which they live? Does family dynamic play a part? Is it cultural? Socioeconomics? Is it tied to physical or mental strength or whether someone has strong faith? Does the answer lie in a person's DNA or psychological makeup? Is it a belief in a higher power, strong will, or is it just luck or fate?

What do **you** think? What do **you** believe? Take a few moments to jot down your thoughts.

_____

_____

_____

_____

_____

_____

If you want to improve the way you respond and react to challenges, it's essential to recognize preconceived notions and acknowledge how they affect your daily thoughts, beliefs, and actions. Before you begin this journey and move forward in the book, take a moment to think about your life and consider a personal challenge or crisis you've faced.

Did you make a conscious decision to keep moving onward and forge through the struggle? Or was it something someone said to you that inspired you to keep going or gave you the strength to overcome?

_____

_____

_____

_____

_____

_____

_____

_____

The results of this exercise will serve as your "baseline beliefs" and will help bring greater awareness to your, often subconscious, thoughts and mental habits. These lifelong habits can either help or harm you and will set you up for success or sabotage. As uncomfortable as it may be, take some time and be honest with yourself as you look inward and reflect. This exercise is a critical investment in your daily happiness and requires your honest participation to truly "reset" what you believe is possible and transform your perspective.

Now that you've checked your "luggage," I invite you to sit back and enjoy this road trip on which we are about to embark. The gas tank is full, and the windows rolled down. Some people, places, and experiences may be familiar to you, while others will be new. Some characters' names have been changed to protect their privacy, but the journey and the incidents are real.

The beauty of this adventure is that it will not only bring you to new places, but it will provide you with a different, greater perspective as you peer through a shared lens. This is a journey of survival, but it's also a roadmap to overcoming self-doubt, realizing your power, discovering your purpose, and achieving inner peace by living the life you envision for yourself—not what others see, expect, or try to force upon you. It's a cathartic quest that gives readers the power, permission, and know-how to leave the past behind and move forward in a positive life full of passion and possibilities.

By the time you reach the end of this book, you may find that your responses to the questions posed earlier differ drastically from when you embarked upon this journey.

Introduction

The product of two lost souls, my existence was destined to be a journey of uncertainty, trial, and error. With a father void of emotion and a mother with an abundance of it, I became a cross between knowing and feeling. Questioning everything, I searched for answers with an insatiable need to understand. Determined to find peace and common ground, I refused to accept that I was simply a product of inherited behaviors and personalities but a mixture of good and bad examples from which to grow and learn.

From the military base where I drew my first breath, strength and resiliency grew amidst an unstable foundation. Like a new recruit suited up for combat and equipped with powerful but unfamiliar weapons, survival became my greatest skill. The absence of firmly planted roots or a traditional, nurturing family catalyzed my self-reliance, adaptability, and appetite for change.

Accustomed to having the rug pulled out from beneath me, I witnessed my parents' unhealthy relationship and experienced the pain of divorce, abandonment, and my mother's illness. From a very young age, different forms of abuse were present in my life. Growing up in the backseat of a Volkswagen bus, life was unpredictable and inconsistent, and I experienced things others my age could never have imagined.

Involuntarily initiated into a mixed life of gypsies, hippies, and radical missionaries, I encountered people and places that changed me for the better, though some, not as much. As I grew older and capable of choosing my path, my unconventional upbringing peeked through, and I embraced my colorful, open-minded spirit. I became a free and fierce energy to reckon with.

I continued chasing the sun, feeding my imagination, embarking on new adventures, and feeling the pull and wonderment of the luminous moon and big sky. While I searched long and hard for genuine and meaningful connections, it was the unavoidable, uncomfortable confrontation of truth I found in being alone that allowed me to truly, and deeply connect to many places and with many people.

I realized that my heightened sense of awareness, along with my willingness to be open and authentic in my relationships, gave me a unique advantage in reaching people and connecting with their hearts.

SECTION 1

Where the Road Begins (Chapters 1-4)

In this section, readers will understand where and how my journey began and will have an opportunity to reflect upon and draw comparisons to their own. With an upbringing that was far from conventional, uninhibited in parenting style, and void of "child proofing," I spent my childhood on the road with a blurred line between figurative and literal reference. For instance, seatbelts were not required, guardrails were often missing, and speed limits were merely suggestions. Life was an experiment meant to be figured out, and looming dangers were met with Band-Aids instead of prevention. Trial and error resulted in the lessons we learned, and pain was the greatest teacher.

The Journey Begins:

Entangled in the words, I finally let go. I gave in to the seductive temptation that had long been calling me. Terrified by the power my words possessed and the emotions they elicited; I couldn't hold onto them any longer. Caressing my pen with a sense of eager hesitation, I placed it on the table and positioned my readied fingers. As they hovered over the keyboard, an overwhelming magnetic force began to draw them closer. My fingers tingling as my mind began to excite, unconsciously entered a secret combination that unlocked the chain protecting my soul's secrets.

With a slow and subtle yet deliberate force of resistant keys, words that I had long-imprisoned rushed out of me, leaving trails of evidence on my cheeks. I stared off for a brief moment and then quickly and completely submerged myself into the place I've always belonged and could never escape. Many times and places joined together and became one. It was the place my purpose patiently awaited and longingly invited me to realize and retrieve.

Fully engulfed and lost in this colorful world of finely articulated expression, I introduced the girl I once was to the woman I had become. It was here, in the place I tried hard to forget, that I found myself again. It was here that I slew many of my doubts, abolished my limitations, and overcame negativity.

In their place, relentless dreams, hopes, and aspirations took shape and found ways to escape and creep into my waking hours. In my mind, questions resolved, mysteries illuminated me, and enlightenment came into focus as I learned to set my words and spirit free.

It was here that I wrestled with demons, dressed the wounds, stitched the dangling pieces of my heart, and discovered purpose in the pain of scars and imperfections. I recognized angels, felt their presence and protection, and in my mind, accepted and appreciated that I was different.

Unable to ignore words that clamored to get out and feelings that begged to be acknowledged, I set them free with a twist of the hand. Words no longer taunted me, daring me to speak.

Instead, I flirtatiously danced with them and learned to make music with major and minor notes. They became happy, exciting, triumphant arrangements, and sad, fearful, and melancholy ones. The collection of them all is what made me who I am. Honest and raw, I now honor this organic creation composed of painful truths and unbelievable beauty.

CHAPTER 1

The End of the Innocence

It was the first day of Spring on a military base in Stuttgart, Germany, and another Army brat was born. The offspring of two restless spirits, I was named after my maternal grandfather, John. My mother chose *Shane*, an anglicized version of the popular Irish name, to honor her father while tying in "schon" (a similar-sounding German word) that means beautiful. My mother, Bernadette, thought it was the perfect balance of masculine and feminine.

My father, Scott, was a member of the First Battalion, Forty-first Field Artillery, and my mother, his new bride, joined him after he was stationed overseas. You could say that I've been "looking up" since the day I was born because I entered this world in breech position, or "butt first," as my mom would say. Back then, C-sections were considered a last resort, and doctors only performed them if there were signs of distress or life-threatening complications. Otherwise, the standard birthing protocol was to bear down and push harder. My mother reminded me of this a time or two.

Bernadette didn't give me a middle name, although she insisted that I had one at my baptism. Unfortunately, she never could recall what it was. She described my godparents as a very nice, older couple whom my parents met after leaving Germany and being stationed in Kentucky. Bernadette lost touch with them sometime after we left the base.

In high school, my mother fell in love with my father—a tall, handsome guy for whom she proudly said she "saved herself." Years later, she would say what a terrible mistake it was to marry Scott. Bernadette was not an overly happy child, from what various family members told me, and she was an even more unhappy teenager.

She told me many stories of her childhood—tales of her father sent off to fight in the war while her mother was left alone to work and care for the kids and the home, stories of how my grandfather, a man of few words, discovered a love of drink, and about the drama and jealousy between Bernadette and her siblings that would later be the cause of even more wars at home. Three of them were born before the war, and three others, including my mom, were born after my grandfather's term of service—products of the seven-year itch. My mother was the middle child and the only girl of the second, post-war batch. The pre-war kids were all girls, so I suppose my mother faced some distinct challenges.

When she was a teenager, Bernadette's parents decided to relocate upstate New York. Although they had previously lived on a farm upstate when she was very young, she (unlike her older siblings) had grown accustomed to a more suburban lifestyle. Bernadette deeply resented that they uprooted her when she was near graduating and moved them back into the country.

This transition affected her profoundly as she often blamed many of her life choices on this upsetting event. Feeling like this move only led her to a dead-end in life, she spent much of her time dreaming about her future. Leaving her friends, many social activities, and "endless" opportunities behind, only to be forced to finish high school in the "sticks," was pivotal and felt more like a punishment. If it weren't for the move, Bernadette believed she would have avoided her biggest mistake altogether—meeting and marrying Scott.

As a teenager, Bernadette was pretty miserable and desperately wanted out of "small-town, USA." She never liked it there, and to this day, she's convinced that people practice black magic in that area because of the deep darkness she felt. She claimed that people were different there, and since everyone knew one another, if you didn't fit in, you never would. I suppose resentment over being there unwillingly and unable to leave contributed to her feelings, but as a self-proclaimed "outsider," she believed that people cast spells on her.

Bernadette was a beautiful young woman with long chestnut hair and big brown eyes, and folks described Scott as a tall, good-looking man with blonde hair and blue eyes. He was one of fourteen brothers and sisters (not counting one or two that died at birth), and my mother, the fifth of six children. As twisted fate would have it, their attraction turned into young love, and their budding romance quickly resulted in marriage. Not long after, Scott was shipped out and sent overseas, and Bernadette was excited to follow him. She welcomed this ticket out of Chenango County.

Weaved throughout their love story, though, was evidence of a mismatch of personalities. If there was one word my mother used most often to describe my father, it was selfish. From the way he handled money, to his personal habits and daily routine, even how he made love to her (unwelcome details that always made my young stomach turn) were all self-serving and egocentric. Maybe it stemmed from having to compete with so many siblings for love, attention, and even basic necessities?

Nevertheless, Bernadette was young and in love, and she enjoyed her time in Germany. She loved the culture, the people, the food, the beautiful views of the city, and as irony would have it, the countryside. It wasn't long after I was born that Scott was reassigned, sent back across the pond, and stationed in Kentucky. They arrived in Germany as a newly married couple and left as parents awaiting their next adventure.

This picture, taken in Stuttgart, Germany, is the only picture I have of the three of us.

When I was older, I received an abbreviated overview of life before my brother, Chris, was born. "You were born, and then your brother came along," my mom said. Perhaps, it was because he was born only two years after me, and the life of a military wife happened fast and without much notice. I think she found it challenging to keep a record of things because change was a way of life and happened frequently.

One story in particular always stuck with me, of a dog we had named Pinto. He was a dachshund who saved my life when I accidentally started a fire in our house on base. I was playing with matches and happened to strike one just right. Within seconds, the drapes and shag carpet caught on fire. My mother told me that Pinto kept barking and running back and forth between the living room where I sat, unaware of the rapidly spreading danger, and the kitchen where she was preparing food, and alerted her of the emergency. When my mom found me, I was sitting in the middle of the living room floor with flames all around me. Remarkably, I escaped with nothing more than a small scar above my eyebrow that still exists as a reminder. The house? Well, that's another story.

Sometime later, our beloved Pinto was hit by a car, and my mother was devastated. It was clear how much she loved him as she proudly expressed how smart, sweet, and devoted he was. Listening to my mom describe him and the deep affection she had, it was apparent they shared a special connection that only deepened with his intuitive rescue effort.

Upon racing Pinto's injured body to my father and pleading with him to rush him to the vet, she watched in horror and disbelief as Scott placed Pinto in the trunk of the car and slammed it shut. She begged him to allow Pinto to rest on her lap so she could comfort him as they made the trip, but he didn't want a mess. Bernadette shared this story with me many times to show me how cold Scott's heart was. Whenever she thought back to that terrible day, she couldn't help but think about how awful it must have been for Pinto to die alone in the trunk of a car.

My mother never shielded me from the truth or attempted to sugarcoat things, regardless of my age. It was almost a rite of passage for me. She reasoned that it was better to know the truth and find out early.

I will never forget when my mother first told me about my father's reaction to the news that she was expecting for the second time. I was just a young girl when she told me. As we were finishing our lunch and I was taking the last bite of my cheeseburger, she said, "Do you know what your father said to me when I told him that I was pregnant again?" Before I could even respond, she proceeded to describe how Scott dropped what he was doing and said, "Oh..." followed by a four-letter word. Holding that last bite in my mouth, as if refusing to swallow it would somehow prevent the truth from being digested, I looked at my mom, and she put her head down.

The blistery sting of Scott's crude response all those years ago remained, and as she reached for the check placed on our table, I could see it in her face. Despite her heartbreak, she knew Chris would feel the real pain. Together, we formed an unspoken alliance always to protect him the way a father should, and ours didn't.

Scott likely demonstrated a similar attitude when he learned they were expecting me. Still, I can't help but think my brother experienced a worse pain growing up with a father void of emotional attachment. I've carried this disappointing awareness with me throughout my life and will admit that it contributed to the less-than-fond impression I had of my father.

As a big sister, I felt an even greater responsibility and desire to protect and defend my little brother. With a tough outer shell and confident facade, I always knew his sensitive heart carried many unresolved and painful feelings on the inside. I recognize that Chris spent much of his younger years searching for something to fill the void our father left.

I managed, but for a young boy, it's different. Despite the overwhelmingly negative evidence I knew about my father, I wanted to make my own determinations and conclusions. The compilations of my personal experiences later in life solidified my early impressions.

Despite Scott's cold and detrimental reaction to Bernadette's pregnancy, life carried on. The days passed by, and her belly grew. Living on a military base, pregnant, and caring for a toddler proved to be trying and lonely for my mom. On my birth certificate, Bernadette's occupation was listed simply as "Housewife." While she cooked and cleaned and managed the house, the view from my playpen offered me many lifelong, valuable lessons as I watched Mr. Rogers.

Days turned into nights, and soon Bernadette was a mother of two. Her time alone at home with a newborn and toddler seemed to increase with each passing day, and Scott's absence was labeled as MIA. My mother told me about the day she desperately pleaded with another man in Scott's service unit to tell her where he was. A very nice gentleman, he periodically checked in on her and occasionally dropped off milk.

He must have felt sorry for her because he eventually handed her a piece of paper with nothing on it but an address. She went to the address and found herself in a trailer park. It was in a doublewide where she found Scott with a woman who, let's just say, matched the description of the expanded trailer where she lived. Bernadette's husband was no longer missing, but he was in action.

Mom's unfiltered description of this experience was just as detailed as others she had shared with me as a young girl. All I could ever think about or feel regarding these mental images was GROSS! Overcome with shock, pain, and disgust, Bernadette took my newborn brother and me back to New York to start a new life as a single mother. Life was not easy for her or us.

Growing up in a single-parent home, we did our back-to-school shopping at Goodwill or Salvation Army. There were no extracurricular activities or sports, and even basic after-school snacks and treats were a huge deal. Our cupboards were stocked strictly with the essentials. If ever there was something "extra" or "special" in our kitchen, we knew not to offer it to a friend because mommy made it very clear that she was "not feeding the neighborhood!"

We grew up eating modest meals—whatever was quick, easy, and inexpensive. Mostly, it was potatoes and vegetables in the crockpot or dishes like tuna casserole. Yuck! There wasn't a whole lot of variety because the income was fixed, and time was scarce. There were a few times that I discovered my mom secretly eating Toblerone chocolate in her bedroom. It was her favorite. The pure delight in her eyes just before she realized she had been caught, is a memory that always makes me smile. We had occasional treats too, but as a mother now myself, I can better understand and appreciate the need for that secret indulgence, and she certainly deserved it.

Some colorful people surrounded us when we were growing up. Being a single mother, I'm sure Bernadette had fewer social networking options to choose from, and it was the 70s, after all. The result—my mom had a lot of obscure friends and acquaintances. They were friendships she formed with people while working at the hair salon, places we frequented, neighbors, and family friends. They ran the gamut from normal and nurturing to eccentric and downright bizarre.

We moved around quite a bit upon returning to New York. Finding a suitable yet affordable place to live with two young children proved to be a challenge. In one multi-family home, I recall being awakened abruptly by a strange man standing over my bed demanding that I give him back his knives! Reeking of cigarettes, he ripped the blankets off my bed as he frantically scoured the room, screaming about his missing knives. "You stole them! Where did you put them? Give me back my knives!"

As I trembled in fear and confusion, my mom entered the bedroom. Illuminated from the hallway light, her silhouette showed a calm but firm stance as she announced, "She doesn't have your knives. You need to leave now." As his wild eyes turned towards her, a suspenseful standoff ensued while she maintained a brave face and asked, "Did you check downstairs? I think you may have put them in a different drawer." Reassuring him that they were downstairs, she guided him to the door. I remember thinking that my mom was unusually calm for such a freak event, and her reaction to this startling episode confused me. I think it may have confused him, too, but also scared him a bit.

The man was another tenant in the home who had a drug problem and was deliriously high when he searched my bed in the middle of the night. My mother didn't appear overly distressed over the event but instead offered him a stern redirection that prompted his departure. She seemed to understand that maintaining control of the situation and taking an authoritative position with him was her only hope. Well played, mom. We didn't live there much longer.

At another multi-apartment home, my mom made friends with a nice man from the apartment just above us. He worked for Entenmanns and often brought extra boxes of cookies home to share with us. Chris and I affectionately referred to him as the "Cookie Monster." He was a kind, respectful Italian man who liked my mom, but I guess he wasn't her type. He was shorter than her (not sure if that had anything to do with it), but I always thought it was such a shame that she didn't connect with him.

Regardless, my brother and I delighted in the special treats, and unlike *some* of my mom's friends, I felt comfortable and at ease around "Cookie." Beyond the tasty gifts, he always noticed my brother and me and greeted us with a big smile and a joke or two. Even after working long days, I could feel the effort and care he put into asking us how school was and if we had a good day. Cookie could have brought us any kind of treat, but he always asked us what our favorites were and if we had any special requests, and he always delivered. I guess you could say it was sort of a fatherly type of protection that I felt. It was in this multi-family home that I felt most safe as a little girl. Our neighbors were friendly, close, and considerate, and we made some great memories there.

One day, the tenants organized and prepared a summer barbecue in the backyard. They prepared food and set up tables. As kids, we were excited for a day of fun and food with our friends and neighbors. It turned out to be a perfect day for a picnic, and the life and laughter that took over the backyard were comforting to me. The barbecue, intended for all residents and guests of residents, had a good turnout.

We played lawn games, grilled food, and enjoyed the great weather and company. I remember feeling happy, and for the first time in a while, like we belonged. We weren't the only kids who had a single parent, and it was a welcome change to be surrounded by others like us.

As I played volleyball with a mixed team of kids and adults, my confidence began to grow, and I felt like we were in a warm and welcoming community. Everyone was laughing and having fun. The weather was perfect, and my mom was happy—something that I always paid attention to and noticed.

Just as I was about to hit the volleyball, a man who was a guest at the party (and had too much to drink) thought it would be funny to pull my elastic waist, terry cloth shorts down as I jumped up. As everyone laughed, I dropped to the ground and nervously tried to cover myself as I pulled my shorts up. I ran off crying in humiliation while my mother undermined the incident as being "no big deal" since "no one saw anything."

I did have underwear on, so she tried to convince me that "he was just playing around." Cookie, however, didn't feel the same and expressed his concern. He made it very clear that it was not funny, nor was it right for him to do that. I can't say for sure, but I think that Cookie Monster may have had a few words with the drunken man.

Between moving around to numerous apartments and adjusting to various living situations, my mom did have some consistent, "stable" friends who would invite us over for regular dinners. The Roccos, a generous Italian family, taught us the tradition of a big Sunday dinner. My mom was friends with their daughter, and I'm confident her parents developed a soft spot for us kids. Homemade "Sunday sauce," as they called it, was a delicious tradition that we loved and anticipated. I even learned how to make the famous secret sauce, but it came at a price as most things do.

The wife, Maria, was warm, kind, and full of kisses, one for each cheek, of course, and always made us feel welcome. She would pull out old toys to play with that she kept from when her kids were younger. Maria always went out of her way to make us feel comfortable, and we certainly never left hungry! The husband, Franco, a timeless Italian man with lots of hair, would have his drink and sit in his easy chair until dinner was ready.

Franco was jolly and loved to tell jokes. "What has two legs but can't walk?" he would ask. "A pair of pants," he snorted. Franco had a contagious smile and a twinkle in his eye, or maybe his eyes were just glassy from the drink. I could say he was something like Santa, even the sitting on his lap part. He enjoyed his food, cocktails, and having lots of company around.

Growing up around Italians, I can say that, traditionally speaking, they are very social, often loud, constantly feeding people, and habitually talking with their hands. I've picked up handwaving while talking along the way, so I strongly advise you to watch your drinks when around me, as I've been known to knock a few over from time to time.

My mother never sat me down and talked to me about girl things or warned me about much in that department. She had more of a "baptism-by-fire" style of parenting that forced me to figure things out on my own. I'm sure that, as a single mother, with a lack of time and energy and having grown up with two brothers instead of sisters, she either didn't know how or didn't want to broach "girl talk."

Bernadette made friends with everyone, so my perception of people was mostly favorable . . . until it wasn't. She taught Chris and me to always be respectful, especially with adults, and never ask for anything when we were at someone's house. Many times, when we went to the Rocco's house, Franco would kiss me hello and ask me to sit on his lap. He was kind, warm, and always interested in what I had to say.

I remember one time, in particular, I felt uncomfortable as he rested his hand on my thigh. He was so subtle and quick about it, and it would happen right in the living room where everyone would congregate, chat, and wait for dinner that I thought it had to have been an accident or an unintentional slip. It got to the point, though, where I disliked going over there and found myself wanting to be in the kitchen more (that's how I learned how to make the sauce!)

But my mom always sent me out of the kitchen to play in the living room with my brother. My initial impression and the correlation I drew of him and Santa (red, full cheeks, inviting, and seemingly harmless smile) quickly changed when I discovered how handsy he was.

Sometime later, I told my mom how Mr. Rocco used to pat my thigh and how I always hated that. To my complete shock and surprise, my mom's response was, "Yeah, he was a dirty old man. He used to do that to me too." I couldn't understand how she could know this about him and willingly allow her daughter to be around him. I later understood that she often made decisions with a means to an end in mind. If the essential goal, i.e., being fed or having a sitter to get to work and make ends meet, meant enduring a pinch of pain, then it wasn't so bad.

Perhaps she didn't think he would be as handsy with me as he was with her, but why take that chance? Was the possibility of insulting her friend's family more important than me? Were we in need of a free meal more than I realized? Was the risk of disrespecting their family more of a concern than the damage it could do to her daughter? Or did she think it wasn't a big deal because she had also experienced it as a child?

I slowly developed a confusing relationship with my mother. Strong and proud, refusing ever to be wrong, outgoing, funny, sensitive, and caring as well, she often did things for strangers and always helped a stray in need—whether an animal or a person. However, her track record of poor judgment and often unhealthy parental guidance led me to question many things. My mom taught me valuable life lessons, but my exposure to some of her "friends" became a communal approach to my instruction that proved to be good and bad.

After moving from place to place, we eventually landed in an eclectic village situated on the Hudson River. We lived smack dab in the center of downtown in an apartment above a deli. The police department was just a few buildings down from where we lived, and the local village diner was around the corner. I have many memories of going to the restaurant where my mom was friends with the owner. She seemed to know everyone and everyone knew her.

Bernadette often introduced us to people by saying, "this is my friend," even if she had only met them once before. At the diner, we often ordered corn muffins. They were big, delicious, and within our budget. Still, we got one toasted and split three ways. It was always perfectly browned with just a slight toasted crisp on the side where it sizzled on the griddle, and the generous pat of butter would slide across it as it slowly melted and soaked into it, giving it a caramelized taste. Mmmmm!

On occasion, the owner gave us an extra one, so we had a little more to enjoy. He watched Chris and me grow up, and his restaurant felt like a second home. My mom chatted with the waitresses as we sat surrounded by "regulars" who also became our friends. The meals we shared as a family at the cozy little downtown diner were always special, never taken for granted, and as comforting and nourishing as the meals we had in our own kitchen.

One of Bernadette's long-time friends, Eve, lived in the same village, and she was a hippie in every sense of the word. She lived life freely and without rules. We went to Eve's house often, and her enthusiasm and zest for life mesmerized me.

One time, after knocking on her door for what felt like forever, she eventually yelled down from upstairs and invited us to "come on in!" As we walked up the staircase of her colorful Victorian home, my mom yelled out her name to locate her. After a few repetitions, Eve responded from inside the bathroom, saying, "I'm in here." I assumed she was working on something in there, but to my surprise, we found her soaking in her tub, unphased and uninhibited. "Oh, hey there," Eve excitedly greeted us as she soaped up her washcloth and continued to scrub her body. "What are you girls up to?"

As a young girl, I remember feeling a little embarrassed and not wanting to stare at her breasts positioned just above the bubbles in her bath, but she just continued to casually talk to us as if that was how all people greeted guests. My mother always acknowledged that her friends were a bit "crazy," but it never stopped her from hanging out with them or allowing her children. I realize now that my mom was crazy too.

Eve always told me stories about fairies and magical things, and it expanded my already inquisitive mind. Her tales filled me with excitement and ignited a deep curiosity and wonderment. With each story, a tingling sensation would spark beautiful imagery and invite comforting thoughts within me. I imagined living in the magical worlds she described and desperately wanted to visit these secret places. I knew in my heart that only those who could feel the enchanting tug of these magical places possessed the power to find them. I knew I felt it.

One winter day, Eve announced that we were going on an adventure. I was so excited I could hardly contain myself. With a smile so wide it hurt my cheeks, I began tapping my feet quickly as I alternated between the left and the right, allowing a happy dance to ensue. Eve said something about ice skating, but that was only half of the story. I have no idea where the skates came from, but I remember she drove quite a while before we arrived at a frozen pond where the trees, covered in snow, were like white canopies framing a wintery wonderland deep in the woods.

The further we walked, the more magical it became. I felt as though we were stepping into a fairy tale. The frozen pond, perfectly untouched, had a light dusting of snow on top. As the birds chirped and little animals rustled about, Eve described the magic of the area we were entering.

Eve whispered, "This is where fairies live, Shane." I held my breath as she pointed to an area just across the pond, "Look! Just there! Did you see her?" As I fixed my eyes on the direction she pointed, I exhaled as my heart beat faster in excitement. As I gazed out with determination to locate the fairy, Eve continued, "only those who truly believe in them can see them and find this place." I knew that I caught a glimpse of a wing and heard the rustle as one fluttered by.

We skated for hours in the magical forest where fairies gleefully watched us. I delighted in the knowledge that they were quietly observing us, and it created a desire in me to put my best foot forward and skate as gracefully and gently as I could. If they listened to me and heard me speak, they would know how much I loved them and how I would keep this place a secret and never ever tell anyone where it was. They could trust me, and I welcomed them to come out and play.

In a few short hours, I was transported to another world—a world of wonder that I carry with me still. A world that I didn't need "proof" to believe in, only a willingness to imagine. I will never forget the magic and wonder that I felt that day and how it changed me. It gave me unending permission to dream, hope, and wish for things—even when others ceased to do so.

As a little girl, a young adult, and a mother, I look back, remembering, and draw from this experience the power of possibilities and the magic I feel when I choose to believe.

The time Eve spent with me igniting my imagination and fueling my wonder is a gift that has transcended many areas of my life. I have faith in God, I believe in miracles, and I feel angels ever-present in my life in part because of these magical moments she shared with me. She had opened a door for me, and when I truly believe, I can see and feel the magic beyond the frame. It was a test to appreciate that which we can see and that which we cannot.

Choosing to believe in goodness, I know that magical moments exist every day if we only stop and look for them. It may not be a magical world of fairies, but I have learned a lot from believing in things that I cannot see or understand.

Play Track 1 (The End of the Innocence – Don Henley) in Broken Little Believer Playlist

Baggage Check:

Do you remember a time in your life when you wish you hadn't seen or heard something? Perhaps it took a piece of your innocence or stole a little bit of "magic" from you. At the same time, was there a time in your life filled with hope and sheer excitement—perhaps something that reminded you of the child within? Do you draw from those feelings and carry them with you? Or have you lost or stored that piece of luggage?

_____

_____

_____

_____

_____

_____

_____

_____

_____

_____

CHAPTER 2

Do I Make You Proud?

I was fortunate to have a close relationship with my maternal grandparents, particularly my grandmother, with whom I shared a birthday. We would often sit and talk for hours about life, family, faith, animals, you name it. While others would grow tired of long talks at the kitchen table over Canadian tea, I reveled in this time with my grandmother. I knew it wouldn't last forever, and I wanted to capture and record every story and memory she shared with me.

My moments with "Memie," as she was infamously known to all of her grandchildren, were precious and filled with many stories, Scrabble games, baking, listening to music, and a lot of me just following her around the house as she did routine housework. I loved to sit in the bathroom and watch her hang the clothes out on the line. I marveled at the pulley system, which ran from the door adjacent to the bathroom to a free-standing post in the yard.

I remember thinking how incredible this contraption was. Memie didn't have to leave her house to hang clothes on the line, and I would watch as she methodically pinned clothes, sheets, and towels on it, and, with each pull of the rope, would hear the squeak of the track as she moved it to the next open space.

Later, when everything was dry (it always depended on the weather temperature, moisture levels, and the amount of wind present that day), I would help her fold. There's nothing quite like the smell of fresh laundry after being hung out on the line and dried by the fresh air and a country breeze.

Memie was strong-minded and soft-hearted. She was a peacekeeper but never shied away from declaring or defending her position. While she believed in God, she was a bit of a radical thinker and often presented evidence of truth in many religions and philosophies. She and my grandfather raised all of their children Catholic, but she also told me that she believed in reincarnation. Memie said that she would come back as a giant oak tree or a squawking crow in her next life.

Two flags flew proudly outside their home in upstate New York—the American flag and the Canadian flag. My grandfather served in the military and defended both countries, so it was only appropriate that both flags would be displayed on the land they loved and called home. My grandmother was born and raised in Canada, where my grandfather served as a member of the Black Watch Army. Of course, you also couldn't help but notice the many green and orange items in and around the house, signifying an Irishman lived there. We called him "Boppie."

My grandmother taught in a one-room schoolhouse in Canada when she was younger. She loved to tell me the story about the time her students locked her in the outhouse and how she screamed from the inside, demanding they let her out.

After marrying my grandfather, an Irish immigrant, they moved to New York. Throughout their life together, they had a farm, owned a snowmobile lodge, and both drove school buses. My grandmother's pictures of her retirement celebration showed Memie surrounded by coworkers in front of a big cake with her name and image of a school bus. Everyone loved and enjoyed being around Memie, and they looked to her for advice or a listening ear.

My grandmother never placed emphasis on material things. She could take something or leave it and made it a habit never to have anything she would be upset over losing. Her attachment and level of commitment were to people and animals. She took in countless cats and dogs that once were pets to people who spent the summers up at the lake but left behind. It's hard to say just how many cats came to know Memie & Boppie's as their home. They were mainly outdoor cats that would only occasionally come inside.

There was Tom Tom who lived the longest and made the biggest impression on me. He was a tomcat my mom picked up when she worked at a gas station. The others were Devil, Stripey, Fluffy, Mommy, Butter, and the names went on and on. With so many cats to feed, Memie had to find ways to stretch the dollar as far as she could. Back then, she used to buy Cat Chow and Meow Mix dry food. One of them had a promotion for a free cat dish. Together, she and I would cut out the backs of boxes and collect the valuable squares that, when mailed in, would get you a free yellow plastic food dish.

Soon, Memie had a tower of yellow dishes stacked in the corner on her kitchen floor. Each morning she pulled them out and began preparing the meal line. If it was nice out, she set the dishes out on the back deck. If it were cold or snowy, she would open the back door and scatter them from the entryway leading to the kitchen, giving each their own space to eat and enjoy.

We could hear the hollow sound of plastic bowls as she unnested them and the "ching" of dry food as she poured kibble into each one. Soon, meows seemed to multiply and become closer until they all gathered around her feet. Although the number of cats fluctuated over the years, one thing never changed, and that was the special gift that always awaited us at the front door. Living so close to the water, the cats would proudly catch and carry fish from the reservoir in their mouths. They made it a habit to leave these stinky gifts outside the front door in appreciation for her love and care.

Memie even cared for the wildlife. Countless raccoons gave birth to babies under Memie's front porch, and she would sprinkle dry cat food to provide them with an easier start. I will never forget when Memie was standing outside in the yard with her polyester pants on, and a baby raccoon happened to crawl up inside her pant leg.

Startled, she screamed as she tried shaking her pant leg to coerce him out but was unsuccessful. As the baby raccoon crawled further up her leg, desperate and not knowing what else to do, she pulled her pants down to release the little guy just as a neighbor happened to drive by and witness my grandmother standing there in her bloomers.

She had a great attitude about things and frequently offered reasons or theories to explain why people were the way they were. When a neighbor complained to her about someone, Memie, who took the time to get to know people more than most, would shine a different light on the person. She had a knack for providing a different perspective.

She valued genuine, loyal people. She didn't care what you looked like, where you were from, how much money you had, or what faith you practiced. Many Jehovah's Witnesses had knocked on her door over the years. While some people would go to great lengths to avoid answering the door to these Watch Tower-distributing disciples, my grandmother welcomed many eager Witnesses into her home, where they would sit and visit for hours at a time.

She was "Memie" to me, but to everyone else outside the family, she was Frances (aka "Fran"). Fran made many cups of tea for countless drop-in, stop-by visitors. Anyone who ever had a cup at Memie's knew very well that one teabag made at least two cups because Canadian tea was stronger! It didn't matter the time of day, or whether she was expecting you or not, she warmly invited people in and made her guests comfortable as they sipped tea and shared various thoughts and beliefs.

Years later, when Memie passed away, multiple "good news spreaders" attended her service and shared their genuine affection and respect for the woman who always opened the door to them and invited them in for some Canadian tea. She knew everyone and was friends with all—including the outcasts and those rejected or misunderstood. If you were good to her, Fran was good to you.

My grandfather was born in Ireland, and after coming to the United States, he proudly served our country. "Jack," as he was known to everyone other than his grandchildren, demonstrated a strength that few would dare to challenge. He had firm beliefs, and he wasn't afraid to defend them. Jack spoke unapologetically, and his words, but even more so, his eyes, filled with deep conviction. My grandfather smoked a pipe, and amidst the swirling smoke, you could catch a grin of contentment. It was his family and the simple pleasures in life that gave him the greatest joy.

We always knew where we stood with Boppie, and even though he sometimes found it difficult to express and accept affection, we saw evidence of his big heart in many forms. While his rolled-up flannel sleeves showed a few tattoos from his time in the military, and his well-worn work boots and newsboy hat (comfortable and practical accessories) may have portrayed a rough exterior, beneath all that was a man who loved people, animals, and helping others.

After his years of service and working various jobs upon returning home, one of his favorite positions was driving a school bus for mentally and physically disabled children. He took pride in caring for these students and ensuring their safety. Best of all, he had a knack at always making them laugh, and he never grew tired of it; nor did they.

As he grew older, he had less to say, but with just one look, you knew exactly how he felt. I would watch him as he sat on the couch with the dog curled up beside him, as he drifted off retelling stories of poverty, war, and different times in his life. Snoring would fill the living room before an abrupt, "Close that fridge!" would startle whoever was standing in front of it, pondering what they wanted to get.

There was no wasting anything in their house. If you took it, you ate it or drank it....all of it. I have many memories of my Boppie. For such a "tough" guy, he accepted all the strays my grandmother allowed in, and his best companion, a chihuahua named Prissy, would be by his side to the very end.

I often write about my grandmother because we were so close, and I still feel her powerful presence. Boppie, on the other hand, was the quiet one, content just sitting on the couch watching everyone else. While we shared many conversations, he was not one for small talk. Our chats were meaningful, serious discussions, and sprinkled in between were a few "Pull my finger" invitations. When Boppie spoke, everyone listened. I feel his contemplative, steady presence as well.

Play Track 2 (Do I Make You Proud – Taylor Hicks) in Broken Little Believer Playlist

Baggage Check:

How are you feeling? Did you need to adjust the temperature or take a moment to stretch your legs? Who influenced you when you were younger? What are some of your favorite memories or takeaways from this chapter?

_____

_____

_____

_____

_____

_____

_____

_____

_____

_____

_____

_____

CHAPTER 3

There Is Love

We lived in a funny community with lots of artists, actors, and hippies. The quaint village was home to the richest of the rich and the poorest of the poor. We were on the affluent side of town but struggled to get by in a rental property, which seemed to exaggerate our plight and made me feel like I stuck out even more.

I remember one of the more popular girls inviting me to a birthday party. She was a pleasant, easy-going girl, although we weren't close friends. I assumed her mom probably made her invite everyone in the class because the request surprised me a bit. When it came time to shop for a birthday gift, my mom took me to the store to pick one out. Good ole' Woolworths. My budget? A whole dollar—and that was before dollar stores existed.

The only thing I could find was a small boxed puzzle, which I loathed and did NOT want to give her, but I had no other options. I mean, what kid wants a puzzle for their birthday? It was also a time when it was typical for kids to open their gifts during the party. "Just great!" I thought. Fortunately for me, the girl was polite enough to say, "thanks," before quickly tossing it aside and moving on to unwrap the next present. I didn't blame my mom. We didn't have the money, so the experience was just another addition to my character-building repertoire.

My mother was working and going to school to become a hairdresser at the time. I accompanied her often, and the school sort of became my home away from home for a while. I sat in the twirling salon chairs and watched her, along with the other hairdressers, perform magic, and sometimes murder, on the many mannequin heads that sat perfectly positioned atop adjustable metal clamped bases.

Occasionally, they would need "live" hair models, which became my job when my mom couldn't find anyone else. I didn't always like the finished product, and often, the progressive styles made me an even easier target at school. Still, I was always a fan of change and loved the exhilarating air of confidence I felt at the hair academy. There was an unspoken philosophy of "no fear" that I felt, coupled with a welcome invitation to take chances and try something new. I loved it! To be a hairdresser was all about risk, reinvention, and constant change. The more radical, the better! It was also a great lesson to me that nothing is ever permanent. Change is good and cathartic. It's remarkable, the power of hair.

Life was smoother sailing, living above the deli, and the three of us managed to make it. I was about six years old when my mom met a guy named Jimmy. He was an Italian construction worker, a few years younger than her. They dated for a while before deciding to marry.

Jimmy was funny, easy to get along with, and accepted my brother and me most importantly. I recall having a birthday party in our tiny apartment, and he made an entrance dressed up as a clown. It wasn't a fancy disguise, but I remember, despite some embarrassment, being touched by his willingness to be the entertainment for the only traditional birthday party I had as a child.

Since it wasn't a fancy costume (it mainly consisted of colorful face makeup), I remember laughing and saying, "I know it's you, Jimmy," to which he made funny clown faces and said, "Who's Jimmy? I'm Chuckles the Clown."

The wedding was a small but sweet affair. I was the flower girl, and my brother, Chris, was the ring bearer. Ira, our upstairs neighbor, provided the music, playing "The Wedding Song" on his guitar during the ceremony. My mother looked beautiful with a simple crown of flowers on her head and wearing a used wedding dress she found at Goodwill.

The reception was an even smaller gathering at a local hall with family and close friends. As the song goes, "there was love." Little did we know that a lyrical question within their wedding song demanded an answer from them sooner than expected—"Is it love that brings you here or love that brings you life?"[2]

Shortly after the wedding, the happy couple departed for their honeymoon. Upon their return, we had plans to move into a bigger space—a rented house in an area with dirt on the ground and space to run around. The house, along with a few other bungalow-style homes, was positioned in a circular-like pattern—a neighborhood within a neighborhood. We could play safely outside with other kids on the cul-de-sac-like road and not worry about traffic.

Chris and I were excited about the move. Until then, my mom left us to stay with Ira during their honeymoon. Ira was a burly guy and single. We didn't know him all that well, so I don't understand why my mom decided to leave an almost seven-year-old girl and a four-year-old boy with a single man when other, more natural, options existed. Perhaps it was just more convenient for school and other routine reasons, or maybe driving us four hours up to our grandparents was not feasible, but as they say, convenience comes at a price.

We brought our things upstairs and said goodbye to our mom and new stepdad. The first day or two was ok. Ira was a musician, so he showed us his instruments, equipment, and how it all worked. We got to use the microphone, and I even got to sing a little with it. Something started to change, though, and I became increasingly uncomfortable as the evenings approached. We would have dinner and watch TV, and all was relatively uneventful—until one night when, as we watched a show, Ira invited me to sit on his lap.

The invitation was warm and friendly, but it soon became more insistent. After declining politely several times, Ira insisted roughly, "Come, sit here!" as he quickly slapped his knee. Reluctantly, I did, as I felt the need to comply with an adult. I had never felt so uncomfortable or awkward as I did sitting on this man's lap. I wasn't a toddler, so it seemed weird to be sitting on someone's lap (unless it was Santa's), and my previous experience at the Rocco's left me feeling even more uncomfortable about it.

As Chris sat engrossed in the TV show on the floor just below me, Ira placed his hand on my knee. This contact sent shivers down my spine. I flinched, and my knee automatically jerked. I sat stiff as a board, feeling cold inside and unsafe. I considered ways to excuse myself as my heart raced faster and faster.

He started to slowly, firmly run his hand up my thigh towards the inside of my leg. I immediately jumped off and sat near my brother. Ira continued to ask me to sit on his lap, and I continued to decline, using the best manners I could muster up.

As it got later, and we were nearing the end of our stay, he excitedly announced that we were going to do something really fun since it was our last night. As he got out some blankets and tossed them in a pile on the floor, he said, "Have you ever made forts out of blankets?"

Chris, delighted by the idea, inquisitively answered, "No, we've never done that! How do you make them?" As Ira got out some chairs and small tables, he pulled my brother closer and showed him how to drape them over the furniture to make "forts." "You and your sister can make forts and sleep in them tonight."

Not nearly as impressed or as excited as my brother, I went along with the idea. "When you're done making your fort, we can get ice cream, and you can eat it in the tents while we watch a movie." Ira's suggestion sounded better to me, and my brother was bouncing off the walls and squealing, "YEAH!" The deli was on the ground floor; we lived on the second, and Ira's apartment was directly above ours on the top floor.

Chris and I were excited about ice cream. The deli had our favorite—a slice of Neapolitan ice cream wedged between two waffles. I can still smell the cellophane mixed with the sweetness of the ice cream as I unwrapped it.

Before I knew it, Ira handed my brother some money and instructed him to go down to the deli and get the ice cream for us. I immediately lunged to grab my brother and said that I had to go with him. I mean, he was only four at the time. But before I could stop him, he was already out the door and heading down the stairs to the deli.

I was anxious and upset because I always watched over my brother, but in a flash, he was gone. Ira stopped me and said, "You've got to take your vitamins first." Everything about that moment scared and confused me while the panic over my brother being alone started to grow. Chris and I both took vitamins regularly, so I didn't think anything of it, but as an adult looking back, I now know the bottles he reached for above the fridge were prescription (likely a sleeping aid).

When I questioned what kind of vitamins he was giving me, he informed me that they were the same kind I took at home, but just in another bottle. "There are lots of different brands, so that's why they look different." In a hurry to get my brother, I took two as he instructed and raced to the door just as Chris returned. The ice cream tasted different to me. It had a weird aftertaste, and my tongue felt strange. The last thing I remember was eating the ice cream waffle.

The next morning, I woke up in a tent made of blankets and found myself completely naked and alone. I was terrified and embarrassed as I cried in silence. I wrapped myself in a nearby blanket and slowly peeked outside the tent. I could see Ira asleep in his bed, and Chris was also sleeping nearby. He was fully clothed and, although I was initially concerned, I didn't get the impression that Ira had touched him.

As fast and quietly as I could, I raced to the bathroom, where I found my underwear, damp and hanging in the shower, with my clothes nearby. My heart was pounding. I felt so helpless, scared, and alone. I didn't feel pain, so when I tried to make sense of this experience later, I don't think he did THAT. However, the thought of what he could have or likely did to me is something I will never know. Did he just look at me? I doubt it. Did he touch and fondle me as I lay sedated? Did he masturbate and leave his mess on me? Is that why my underwear was damp and hanging in the bathroom? Was he on top of me? Did he kiss me?

I felt disgusting and ashamed, and yet I didn't even know what exactly I should be ashamed of. I only knew that I had been sexually abused and was utterly helpless and powerless. I often wonder if it was a blessing to be spared the memory of Ira's actions, but not knowing what happened has been even more painful in some ways. The mystery of what he did to me left me feeling completely unaware of a part of my life in which no amount of searching for answers would ever bring understanding. He found pleasure in abusing me, and I had no choice in the matter.

I don't know what happened next, but I do remember my mom and Jimmy coming home soon after to pick us up, and it was then that I knew something else was wrong. I prepared to tell my mom what happened. My breath was shallow, and I felt like I was going to hyperventilate. I was scared but relieved that she was home to tell her what had happened finally.

We got home, walked through the front door, and I blurted out, "Mom, I have to tell you something," but with a serious and frightened look on her face, she directed me to sit on her bed and said, "First, I need to talk to you about something very important." I was convinced that somehow, she found out about what happened and was going to offer me solace, but as she drew closer, I knew that was not the case.

As she struggled with how to begin, I noticed bruises on her arms and legs, and I quickly grew scared by her seriousness and the new marks I observed on her body. She told me that she became ill while they were on their honeymoon and went to the hospital. They did blood work and discovered that she had something called leukemia.

She told me that I needed to be brave and take care of my brother. The doctors did not give her a lot of hope or time because she had an aggressive cancer—acute myeloid leukemia or AML.

Having felt as though I was going to hyperventilate when I thought of sharing what had happened to me, I was now breathing even more rapidly and feeling as though I couldn't catch my breath. It felt like a terrible nightmare, and I wanted to wake up. I cried as I insisted, "The doctors are wrong. You're going to be okay, mom. You have to be."

She didn't agree with me as I expected her to and instead maintained a tough facade. She did not assure me of anything. She did not make any promises. Being sick was not like my mom. Being emotionless was not like her either. Bernadette was invincible and more transparent than any other woman I knew. But she simply told me that I needed to be brave and take care of my brother, Chris.

Her journey began at Memorial Sloan Kettering Hospital, where she underwent several excruciating bone marrow biopsies. She told me about the size of the needles and how scared she was when she saw them, knowing they would be inserted into her spine. A nurse told her to turn around and assured her, "it won't hurt," but the nurse lied. My mom later told me how she cried and screamed out in pain. Results from these tests precipitated her discharge from the hospital along with a hopeless, "We're sorry, but there's nothing more we can do for you."

Life as we knew it crumbled all around us. Adults made plans, and we said, "I love you" over and over again. Mom gave me countless instructions regarding caring for my brother. "Help him with school. Be sure he takes a bath and brushes his teeth. He's going to need your help, Shane. You're his big sister."

Weeping, she bombarded me with instructions I must never forget, like "I love you so much, don't worry, pray hard, and never lose faith." I could tell that she was fighting back the tears as she went down a mental list of everything she wanted to say, so I knew it was important to listen intently.

I had so many questions as I frantically asked, "But where are you going? Who are we going to stay with? How long will you be gone?" It was one of the darkest times in our lives. Each time I cried to my mom, "I don't want you to die," she would tell me that I needed to be strong and brave. Jimmy had heard about a research hospital in Seattle that was doing trial therapies and treatments. It was their only hope.

For being such a short stay, that little bungalow sure did hold a lot of memories. It was there that I remember my mom sitting me down on her bed in the front room as she held back tears and told me that she was sick. I don't know all the details of our subsequent plans. Still, I recall every piece of furniture in the room, the pictures I stared at, the color of the drapes, the many shades of black and blue that were visible on my mom's body, and every other little detail of that front bedroom where life changed.

We packed up quickly—our time in that little house would soon be over. We were going to our grandparents while my mom and stepfather would make the trek to Seattle for an experimental treatment. Ironically, Jimmy heard about the treatment through someone in his family and shared it with my mom. Could it be love that would bring her life?

With limited money, they headed west. We didn't know how long our parents would be gone or what they would do, but we all prayed that it wouldn't be long and that it would work. It was her only chance and our last hope. I cried and cried as we said goodbye, wondering if it would be the last time we would ever see her.

*Play Track 3 (Wedding Song (There Is Love) –
Noel Paul Stookey) in Broken Little Believer Playlist*

Baggage Check:

Is there a pain from your past that you carry with you and can't seem to put down?

_____

_____

_____

_____

_____

_____

_____

_____

_____

_____

_____

_____

CHAPTER 4

Everything I Own

Living with our grandparents, Chris and I attended Catholic school. Each day, we walked a few hundred feet from Memie and Boppie's house to the wooden, handmade shelter and would wait for a bus to come down the dusty, dirt road. The tiny hut looked a little like an outhouse with a bench in it and only fit two to three people, but it shielded us from the elements. The memory brings back a comforting feeling I felt during some upsetting times.

Being upstate was a positive experience in light of our sad and scary circumstances. Fresh air, freedom of the outdoors, and the many adventures I found in nature were good for my soul. It kept me looking for beauty and goodness while providing me with the quiet stillness I needed. The peaceful and serene surrounding was just what my contemplative, busy mind required.

On the flip side, it was also at this time in my life that I developed a love of boxing as I'd sit with my grandfather on the couch and watch late-night matches with him on TV. It was our thing, and it complimented my very distinct thoughtful and sensitive side.

While watching some of the biggest and best boxers, I learned that life itself is a lot like a good fight. When the pressure is on, and everything is at stake, you need to protect yourself, be quick on your feet, be ready for unexpected jabs and uppercuts, and you must possess not only physical strength but the mental strength to dig down deep, grab hold of your will, get back up, and keep fighting. In and out of the ring, I've learned a true champion isn't always the one who wins a fight, but the one who continues to take hits while maintaining grace—regardless of the judge's decision.

Attending Catholic school was also good practice, as I learned to channel the sting of a few ruler slaps on the hand and turned it into greater drive and renewed commitment. I learned to achieve my aspirations without talking back to the teachers and maintaining respect no matter what.

Sadly, the news came back that my mom was not doing well, and the treatments were not working. Memie, meaning well, shared this news with someone on my biological father's side. With so many siblings, and the majority living in the same area as my mom's parents, word traveled fast. Scott had not been part of our lives before this, so I had imagined that perhaps others envisioned him being a hero who would ride in and save us from this tragic experience, but that wasn't what I believed.

My mom was distraught that Memie involved Scott and was worried about our future should he get involved. She immediately asked her sister Jeannie, who also lived on the hill near my grandparents, if she would take us. My aunt and her husband agreed to allow us to stay with them until she was well enough to come and get us.

They lived in a small farmhouse on some property with a barn out back where my uncle took care of his animals. Here, I learned more about farm life and discovered all the things that happen in barns. The cute animals I once fed and gave names would eventually be dinner. My heart broke when I first learned this, but that was how we ate. My uncle was a kind and gentle man, and he taught me about farm living in the most humane way possible.

Our stay at our Aunt Jeannie's didn't last long. There was a knock on the door one day, and we overheard Memie telling my aunt that we belonged with our father, "considering the circumstances and Bernadette's chances of surviving." Jeannie had given my mother her word that she would never freely hand us over to our estranged father. From under the bed where we hid, I listened to their conversation at the door as Jeannie told Memie we were out playing with kids down the road. "Their father will be coming to get them," Memie said as she walked away, and as soon as the door closed, a covert operation was soon underway.

"You can come out now," Aunt Jeannie whispered as she stood over the twin bed where Chris and I were hiding. "She's gone, but we need to hurry." She raced around the house, picking up articles of clothing and necessities, and packed some food for a trip. I don't know how the plan came together so quickly, but we left as suddenly as we had arrived, each with a bag of clothes and a brown paper bag filled with a sandwich and a drink.

My aunt drove us to the bus stop where we boarded a Greyhound bus late in the day. The hurried instructions—"Do not get off until you're told to, and stay close to your brother." It wasn't an unusual request of me as a little girl to watch over Chris. I had been his protector for some time.

I helped my five-year-old brother up the bus steps, said hello to the driver, and took two front seats opposite the driver. Now positioned high above Aunt Jeannie, standing outside just below my window, we waved goodbye as the bus pulled away. Chris asked me a million questions; "Where are we going?" How long till we get there? Will mommy be there?" I didn't have any answers. The trip seemed to take forever as the day soon turned to night. I didn't know where in New Jersey we were heading, but I knew it was where our new step-grandparents lived. It was the middle of the night when we arrived, and I nudged my brother. "Wake up, Chris. We're here."

As we made our way off the bus, the driver looked at me and said, "You take care, young lady." It's funny the things you remember. Standing there, our new grandparents looked relieved and happy, yet a little nervous about receiving us. We didn't know each other that well. Our mom had just married their son a few months earlier. Retired and enjoying the luxuries of an adult community, their South Jersey condo was a dream come true. They were kind and welcoming, but I could sense fear and concern behind their smiles.

Their home was the closest thing to a museum I had ever seen. It was beautifully decorated, and the crisp, clean furniture was an off-white color. I immediately observed the fragility of the décor, including plenty of glass and crystal. It was clear they were enjoying retirement before two young kids showed up at their front steps.

Their pride in having a sophisticated, well-kept home was evident and now in jeopardy. Their children were all adults, and all but one had since moved out. This arrangement would be an adjustment for everyone. They were friendly, accommodating, and offered us a lot of food—Italians are like that. It was a far cry from life in the country. Food came from the store, not the barn or garden. My new grandmother showed me around their townhouse, pointed out where we would sleep, where the kitchen was, and how to find the bathroom.

The next day, they enrolled us in school. I was nervous. I didn't know anyone, and I worried about my mom. My first impression of the school was that it was big, bright, and fancy. Coming from Catholic school, it seemed to have a little extra sparkle and shine. I made a few friends and was excited about some activities I was invited to attend.

The adjustment was relatively quick and easy, and I enjoyed this new experience that had initially seemed so scary. I took the bus home with a sense of relief, feeling as though everything on our end was working out so far. As the school bus approached our stop, my sense of relief toppled out the window. I stood up as it rolled to a halt, immediately noticing several police cars parked outside my grandparent's townhouse.

It was a gated community, so my grandmother was standing just outside of the main entrance as she waited for the school bus. I couldn't help but look past her and focus on all the activity behind her. Lights were flashing as several police officers stood outside the condo talking to my grandfather. My grandmother saw the panic in my eyes, and I could see concern in hers. I was sick to my stomach thinking about what could be wrong, but after realizing all the bus occupants had observed the new kid get off the bus to a SWAT team that appeared to be awaiting her, embarrassment also set in.

The attempt to hide us from our biological father was foiled after attending school in New Jersey for just a few short days. I ran past the police officers and headed straight into my grandparents' house with Grandmother right behind me. She handed me the phone that was resting with the receiver face down as if a conversation had been put on hold. "It's your mom. She wants to talk to you," she said.

I was initially relieved that my mom was on the phone and believed that all was okay. But my relief turned to tears as she told me that she had no choice but to let him take us. "Whose taking us? Taking us where?" I cried as confusion grew. My father was awarded temporary custody of us in light of mom's worsening condition. She promised me on the phone that she would get better and would come and get us as soon as she could.

It's fascinating how memories can blur yet seem crystal clear at the same time. I cried and cried as the police officers coordinated things; the red and blue lights swirled as my new grandparents tearfully packed up our things and hugged us goodbye. Reluctantly and with trepidation, I walked out the front door with my little brother in hand, and that's when I saw him standing there.

Scott was tall with blonde hair, just as Mom had described him. Wearing western-style boots, fitted jeans, and an old t-shirt, he kneeled down on the path of their walkway, and as everyone stood back, still in my peripheral view, he extended his arms out as if he expected or hoped that I would run to him and we would lock into a loving embrace. He disgusted me, and I didn't even know him.

The officers scrambled to assist with the introduction and said, "You don't have to be afraid. This is your dad." But I was afraid. I couldn't even make eye contact. To me, he was the enemy, and the police were helping him load us and our things into his pickup truck. Having no choice but to accept our fate, I sat in the passenger seat and stared outside the window. I didn't want to talk to him. I didn't even want to look at him. He was taking us away, and we had no idea where we were going.

We soon learned that we were heading to Nebraska. We were bound for a little town in the middle of nowhere in a pickup truck with a stranger who called himself "Dad." He wasn't my dad, so with resolve, I sat quietly and stared angrily out the window mile after mile. With my back turned towards him and my shoulders stiffly facing the passenger window beside me, I refused to reposition myself, even when it became painful. My brother was young, so Scott quickly and easily won him over with candy and a few matchbox cars, but not me. I refused to talk to him the entire ride. Even when I had to go to the bathroom, I held it until it hurt. This man was a complete stranger, and he was forcing me to live with him.

After a long, resentful, and uncomfortable drive, we arrived in a small, remote town and neared the blockhouse he called his home. I recall pulling into the driveway and entering through the back door, leading directly into the kitchen. A small dining table sat at the edge of the living room off the tiny kitchen. To the right were the bedrooms and one bathroom. That was it—just a square box of a house. It was a bachelor pad with clothes and overflowing ashtrays strewn about, Playboy magazines stacked on the toilet tank, no food in the kitchen, only empty beer bottles, and certainly no warm and inviting decor.

He enrolled us in school, and we started over again. He worked nights for the railroad, so he slept most of the day. I made dinner from what I could find and tended to my brother. In the morning, I fed him, helped him get dressed, and we walked to school. A few hundred feet away, across the street from the house, was a little country church. I felt compelled to go in.

In Nebraska back then, many churches remained unlocked and were open day and night, so I went there often. Sometimes I just wanted to be alone and think. Most of the time, I sat in a pew and prayed that God would heal my mom and bring her to us. It must have been strange for a small rural community to find a young girl sitting alone in their church. As it turned out, many people did wonder who this little girl was, where she came from, and what her story was.

Little by little, our story unfolded, and the church community warmly welcomed Chris and me. They invited us to various church dinners and activities—another one of God's blessings; they fed us. I received my very first Bible from this tiny church. It was also there that I experienced one of many miracles in which God's grace and protection surrounded me during my life, presented and delivered by loving, caring strangers.

People I didn't even know shared the power of faith and taught me how it looked and felt. While this should have been one of the saddest Christmases for me, away from my dying mother and trying to survive in an environment void of structure, empathy, and compassion, I found all these things in that little church and the people within it. They invited us to go Christmas caroling with the church and created magical moments for us.

Here we were, two young kids facing circumstances that many never knew about, excited to go caroling. On a trailer loaded with bales of hay where we sat, a pickup truck pulled us through town with the spirit of Christmas overflowing. Bundled up and holding cups of hot cocoa as the snowflakes fell, we sang carols in a spiritual experience that I will never forget. We sang for the lonely, the sad, the poor, the unexpecting. As we sang, I found happiness and peace that has stayed with me throughout my life. It's true that in giving, we receive. At eight years old, I discovered Christmas's true spirit and swore that I would never forget it.

I wanted to send my mom a gift for Christmas. It had to be special. As I thought about all the things I wanted to give her but couldn't afford, I decided to make her something from the heart. I found two pieces of wood and nailed them together to form a cross and asked Scott if he would mail it to my mom in the hospital for me. He agreed and told me he sent it.

It was in the little church that I wanted desperately to have and keep a closer relationship with God. No one ever taught me how to pray, per se. I just learned to talk to Him. I asked Him a lot of questions, and sometimes, I even got mad at Him. "Why would you take my mom away from me? She doesn't deserve to be in pain, and we don't deserve to be here!" I made deals with God and bargained for my mom's life. I promised I would do whatever I could if only He would spare her. "Please, God, if you let her live, I will do whatever you ask of me. I will never doubt you or your power. Please, please save my mom!"

As I sat alone in the church one night as I often did, I had a lengthy conversation with God. I walked up to the altar and stood at the podium. As I looked out at the little church, the empty pews, and then down at a hymnal, I noticed a bowl of Eucharist (communion) sitting on a small wooden shelf built into the podium. I wanted to taste it, and I debated with myself over taking a piece.

I wanted to know if it held power and if I would find comfort if I ate it. I wondered if taking it would be a sin. I picked up a piece of bread and stared at it for a bit. I held it in my hand and knew what it represented. Although it was small, it felt warm and familiar. It was something I had longed for, something I wanted to taste and experience. I stood there for quite some time, perplexed and confused. I couldn't resist, so I took the piece of bread. It didn't taste as I had imagined (it was bland and dry), but I savored every bite and held it in my mouth for as long as I could before swallowing it.

My first taste and experience with the Eucharist were more meaningful and memorable to me that night than when I received it later during my First Holy Communion. I had no fancy dress on, and no one surrounded me. The invitation was not extended to me by a priest or minister, and it didn't represent any ritual or rite of passage, but it was a calling to come to the Lord and feel His love and presence in my time of loneliness.

That single unaccounted Eucharist was taken, but not for granted. I hoped it would save me and that God would forgive me for stealing the bread, His body. I didn't realize then how hungry I was for nourishment of many kinds. God fed me, and His spirit sustained me.

The time my brother and I spent with our father was limited, but I began to form my own opinions of him instead of going by what my mother told me. I'm sure that it was an adjustment for him to go from being a bachelor to a father

with two young kids living in the house. We sort of just cohab-
itated, and while he may have tried, I didn't feel he loved us.

He wasn't much of a talker. He would have his coffee,
smoke his cigarette, and often go out to the garage and work
on his truck. That left me free to wander down to the church
and to friends' houses. He had many girl "friends" and, on
occasion, we would go to their places. He always presented
it to us as something fun, playing with other kids and having
dinner at someone else's house.

Somehow, I always found myself being the babysitter to
the other kids while he "talked" to his friend in her bedroom.
We would have dinner and watch TV, and later, he would
come out of the bedroom and announce that it was time to
go home. Disgusted by the hints of activity, I kept praying
every day for a miracle for my mom. He knew that I loved
her very much and that my allegiance was to my mom. I'm
sure it upset him to know he could never replace her and that
I was resistant to his involvement in our lives.

Nebraska beef jerky is the best. I recall eating my very
first piece, a long, leathery, jagged-edged, belt-like strip of
protein that I pulled from a giant glass barrel, almost like a
super-sized mason jar. A single piece took a long time to eat,
and my jaws got a workout, but it was so good! After the jerky
was gone, I kept the glass jar in my room and put my change
in it. I would repeatedly pour the coins out on my bed and
count them. I did this most often when I missed my mom
and felt helpless.

This exercise made me feel empowered and signified my
refusal ever to give up hope or stop believing in miracles. I
was saving money to buy bus tickets for Chris and me to leave
that place, and each time I poured the jar of change out, I
wanted to remind my father of that, whether I proclaimed it
aloud or not. Scott knew what the sound of swirling change
meant, and he often laughed at it, which only made me want

to count it over and over again. A few times, he even contributed to my fund.

I was never intentionally mean to Scott. I just never warmed up to him, and he never tried to build a relationship with me. The Christmas I made the cross for my mom, I bought him a deck of cards and wrapped it for him. Maybe it wasn't the best gift, but I tried. It seems ironic to me now that I bought him a deck of cards. It was all I could afford with the couple of dollars I had, but what a hand life dealt all of us.

Many long months passed with no communication from my mom, and I questioned if we would ever see her again. One day, Chris, who was playing in the backyard, came running inside screaming. Startled, I jumped up. "What's wrong?" I shouted back. I thought he was hurt. He continued to holler and repeat over and over again, "Mommy's here! Mommy's here!"

"That's not funny. Don't be a jerk!" It's not nice to lie and make up stupid stories like that, Chris."

"Just come outside and see," he insisted. I made my way through the tiny kitchen and out the back door, and as I rounded the corner of the house to the driveway, I saw my mom. She was bald, skinny, and very pale, standing there with my stepfather, Jimmy. I couldn't believe my eyes, and with happy tears streaming down my face, I ran to my mother.

By God's grace and mercy, my mom was one of the first patients to survive the new and experimental bone marrow transplant procedure. Patients on the same floor with her in the hospital lost their battles, one by one, while she waited and prayed for her bone marrow transplant, donated by one of her sisters, to take.

My mother was one of the lucky few, though I learned later she almost wasn't, having had a near-death experience from which she wasn't expected to return. She shared with me, in great detail, her visions of it and the overwhelming sense of peace she felt. The ultimate reason she couldn't let go had a profound effect on me. It was sometime later that she described how her hospital bed was near the window, and from it, a warm light entered her room. As she got up and walked towards it, the closer she got to it, the more beautiful it was. She recounted every detail of it and said that it was the most beautiful feeling she had ever experienced. She knew the light was calling her home, and she wanted to go to it, but as she stood near the window, she glanced back and saw her lifeless body lying on the bed. At that moment, she turned and walked back to her bed, sat down, and knew that she couldn't leave us with him.

Now my mother was here, standing before us in the driveway. We had endless questions for each other, but after all the hugging, crying, and staring at each other, she asked my father, who was working on his truck in the backyard, if they could take us out for dinner.

"Yeah, I guess," he said. So, off we went in a powder blue Volkswagen van. "Oh my gosh, your hair! Chris, it got so long!" my mom kept saying over and over again. I could feel her staring at me as she remarked, "I can't get over how big you got! You're like a little woman."

We had so many questions for her. "So, what happened? Are you all better now? What did you think of the cross I made for you?" I excitedly asked.

"What cross?" she answered.

"I made you a cross and asked Scott to mail it to you." Without saying a word, we just looked at each other with a look of disgust, knowing he never mailed it.

"We need to discuss what we're going to do now," Mom said. "It's important, and we don't have a lot of time. We need to get back to New York and go before the judge to regain custody of you two."

"What? What do you mean? Do you mean we aren't leaving with you?" I said in a panicked voice. My brother and I both began to cry as we pleaded with her not to leave us. "Why can't we just go with you now? We don't want to go back there!"

She looked at Jimmy, and he looked at her, and without saying a word to each other, she announced with resolve, "Yeah, I'm not leaving you. We'll figure the court thing out later." She didn't need to be convinced to do the right thing. It was a short conversation before she emphatically declared, "We're leaving," and without turning back, we left straight from the restaurant and headed east.

A photo booth picture of me and my mom captured our happy reunion.

Play Track 4 (Everything I Own – Bread) in Broken Little Believer Playlist

Baggage Check:

Can you relate to any of the experiences in this chapter? Have you experienced separation or the loss of a parent or significant other? What sustained you? Was it your faith? Hope? Reflect on this time here.

_____

_____

_____

_____

_____

_____

_____

_____

_____

_____

_____

_____

SECTION 2

Destination Unknown

Spending much of my life traveling across the country in a cramped VW bus, I learned that life was an adventure. Never knowing what the next day would bring or what a new destination held, I share in this section how my life of continual change and unpredictability created wonder and awareness of all that surrounded me. Studying people and places and dissecting experiences was a way of life as I navigated through adolescence and tried to make sense of the world. This section illustrates how instability, lost signals, breakdowns, flat tires, and even a few hitchhikers helped me see the world differently than most. I welcomed new experiences and found ways to make the best out of every situation.

CHAPTER 5

Angels or Los Angeles

With nothing but the shirts on our backs and a full tank of gas, we headed out on a path, not knowing where it might lead or what we might find, but we were happy, and we were together. We drove, ate, and slept in that blue Volkswagen bus with a white top and tied back curtains on the windows.

We made frequent stops so my stepdad could pick up a quick job to earn some gas money, and then we would be back on our way. There were times when it was difficult for all of us to sleep in the van, or we were low on money and couldn't afford gas, so we stopped at shelters and stood in line for cots to sleep on.

We stayed in a few shelters for only one night at a time out of desperation; then, we were back on our way. At times, when we were all jammed into the bus together, there was no room to move. When it was warm out, we camped. Two of us would sleep in the bus, and two would sleep in the tent Jimmy picked up at a discount store. It served us well for several years. Whether in the bus or under the pitched roof of our tent, home was where we made it, and we were happy to be together.

The only things we had for sure were faith and each other. We didn't always know where we were going, where our next meal would come from, or how we would fill the gas tank, but with each experience, we were grateful and felt God's hand and protection over us. We prayed a lot and always thanked God for what we had.

My mother had beaten the odds, and we did not, for a second, take that for granted. God answered our prayers. We didn't need anything more than that. Being a family of strong faith and having much to be grateful for, I remember stopping at a few Catholic churches along the way. We would attend mass here and there, but my mom would often just go in and ask to speak to a priest for a bit.

Perhaps it was her way of repaying her debt or showing gratitude, or maybe it was a way for Mom to sustain her strength, but we never talked about it. We only knew she always felt better when she came out. One time she returned to the van with sandwiches someone had given her for us to eat. She must have been embarrassed as a self-reliant and proud woman, but she accepted the kindness, knowing we needed it and would appreciate it. She vowed to repay the gift.

Our travels brought us back to New York, and we settled into life again. However, when we returned, something just didn't feel quite right to my mom and my stepdad. I don't know if it was all the memories or if they just wanted a new, fresh start, but they quickly decided to move again. They discussed California, among other places.

Of course, it was an adventure-filled trip in the Volkswagen again, and from it, we saw many states in our country and developed a new appreciation and perspective. We were in no hurry to get to California and took our time stopping in various places to try them out for a bit while Jimmy worked at construction sites and took on odd jobs. I attended so many schools I can't remember all their names. It became second nature to stand up before a class and introduce myself as the new student. I enjoyed meeting people, was instinctively curious, appreciative of change and different ways of life.

Somewhere along the way, they decided to give Florida a try. Instead of shooting across the country, we went South and landed in St. Augustine. We lived in a home on stilts, and in the backyard, we would find an occasional alligator that strayed from one of the many bodies of water that surrounded us. Most houses on the shores of the ocean, bay, or swamp areas were on stilts because of rising and receding tides and the presence of snakes and gators.

I loved this particular home because it felt like we were living in a tree fort. We would park our bus underneath the house, which served as a carport, and then go up the stairs to the house. There was a wraparound porch that my brother and I ran and played on, and from a tall palm tree next to us, we would jump on it from the deck and climb down.

This trick was one of my favorite memories of living in that house until that last climb. My brother jumped over the rail, grabbed a big limb, and shimmied down. As I jumped across and held the same palm that I had clung onto many, many times before, it snapped. I fell from the top of the deck all the way down to the ground, flat on my back.

As I laid there, Chris unaware and already running back up the stairs to do it again, I remember fearing that I would die. I tried not to panic, but I couldn't catch my breath, and I didn't have enough air to yell for help. I just kept repeating in my mind. *I don't want to die now.*

When Chris finally saw me lying at the bottom, he began screaming, "Mom! Jimmy! Shanie fell off the deck! I don't know if she's breathing! She's not talking!" It was silent other than his frantic screams for help until finally, I heard my mom terrifyingly yell in response, "What? Where is she?" I imagined he must have pointed down because all I heard next were her fast footsteps coming down the stairway until, finally, I saw her out of the corner of my eye.

Every time I breathed in, it became harder for me to take the next breath. I remember feeling helpless as I lay on the ground waiting for help to arrive, and although the presence of my mom was comforting, her uncertainty of what to do for me only exaggerated my fear.

She took me inside as I continued to gasp for air. Still unable to get words out and with wild eyes growing in desperation, I panicked as Jimmy argued with Mom over whether or not I should go to the hospital. Jimmy was convinced I was okay and said, "She just got the wind knocked out of her. She'll be fine."

But my mom, concerned that my breathing wasn't getting any better, decided to take me in. I did have the wind knocked out of me, and much to my relief, they prepared to hook me up to oxygen in the emergency room. I was afraid it wouldn't come soon enough. As my mom tried her best to describe what happened and answer the many questions the doctor asked her, I wanted to scream, "I need oxygen! Quick!" but couldn't.

When the mask was finally placed on my face, I was surprised by how long it took to feel relief and to get air flowing in my lungs without restriction again. This ordeal terrified me. I had also injured my back and would learn to live with pain.

My brother and I attended public school in Florida, and when my teacher failed to give me a hall pass to go to the restroom, it was then that my mom discovered they still practiced corporal punishment. After mistakenly being sent to the principal's office by a hall monitor, I was forced to lean over a wooden chair, place my hands on the arms of it, and take my three penalty paddles. I don't think the principal had ever met an angry woman from New York until that day, and I don't believe he soon forgot her.

Chris and I rode the bus to and from school. The other children often picked on us because of our shabby, out-of-style clothes. The new kid, I was an easy target in the neighborhood for those with already-formed friendship bonds. I was the odd girl out. The walk home from the bus stop was pure misery.

Every day, a group of kids slowly walked behind me, having fun tormenting me. They called me names, threw sticks, took my backpack, and laughed at me as I tried to walk ahead of them. "Eww...look at her clothes. Where did she get that outfit? She thinks she looks good! Haha," they snickered and giggled. "Oh, and her hair! Gross!"

Depending on the day, I would either come home crying or angry about the mean kids' actions. I think Jimmy got tired of hearing my complaints and suggested I "end it."

"End it? How do I do that?"

My stepdad, very matter-of-factly, said I needed to take on the leader of the group—the one who instigated it all. That sounded a little scary to me, but I was interested in learning more. How would I go about doing this when they were always together, outnumbering me? As he suggested different ways to accomplish this, the ideas started rolling around in my head. With Jimmy's help, a plan began to take shape.

I don't know if these things happen in other families, but I took notes from my Italian stepfather as he laid out what to do. He didn't brush his nose with his thumb, but I felt like he initiated me into a confident, more capable club.

"The first step," he said, "is to get the head bully alone. Tell her you have something you would like to give her. She'll be taken off guard by your niceness, and then when she comes over, knock her out! It's that easy!"

It took some convincing as every day I chickened out, playing the *what-if this happens?* scenarios, but as the torment continued, I realized that I had no choice.

To my surprise, the day I finally acted, she took the bait and followed me home to receive the "gift" I had for her. I invited her into my room and began going through my drawers, pretending to look for something. "Gosh, where did I put it?" I said out loud as I rustled through my drawers. I was so nervous I didn't know what to do, and as I stalled, I could see excitement and anticipation in her eyes, something that made me feel sorry for her.

As I struggled with what to do next, she said, "Well, what is it? Maybe I can help you find it?" leaning in, offering to help me look. I struggled with responding to her, and my emotions went from being angry at her to pitying her.

I excused myself from my room and went to the living room. "I don't know if I can do it," I announced to my stepfather. Confused by the inner conflict I was experiencing, he confidently said, "Just hit her!" I went back into my room, where she was patiently waiting, and I declared, "I don't have anything for you."

Her eyes big, filling with a squirrely nervousness, she jumped up as I informed her that I wanted to fight her for all she had done to me. She then darted for the door as I attempted to block her. After squeezing through and running out of the house, I ran to the door and yelled out after her that there would be no warning if she ever bothered me again.

I was proud of myself for that comment and happy that I didn't stoop to her level, but this experience showed me I have a high threshold for bullshit. Once I hit that threshold, though, there is no more feeling sorry for the other person. I don't know what happened after that, other than my walks from the bus stop were not as bad, but I do know that she and I never looked at each other the same way again.

I made my "official" First Holy Communion in Florida. I wore a simple white dress my Mom found at Goodwill and a headband with a modest and understated lace veil attached. I felt pretty on this special day.

We spent Christmas in our high house, and my all-time favorite present was a homemade dollhouse Jimmy made. Below us, in the carport area, he secretly built and painted it in the evenings after many long workdays. It had several bedrooms on the second floor, and all the living areas were spacious and filled with windows. It was not only the first dollhouse I had ever had, but it was a dream come true. It symbolized everything that I ever wanted and everything that brought me joy: a home with lots of love and space for all. Knowing that he made it for me made it special, and I loved playing with it.

We left Florida and found ourselves back on the road. We crammed everything we owned into that VW bus—including my dollhouse. Our parents told us we could each keep one thing besides our necessities, and I chose Jimmy's handmade gift. As the days went by, we became more and more cramped, and it was increasingly difficult not only to travel with such a bulky item but to find creative ways to sleep around it.

During the night, my brother and I were kicking each other and arguing as siblings do over who was invading whose space. It wasn't just space but patience that was wearing thin. Mom and Jimmy were talking up front, and I heard the word "dollhouse" a few times. My stepfather pulled over on the side of the highway, and my mom, visibly disappointed, told me we needed to let it go. "What? What do you mean?" I asked.

It was a difficult decision, but there was no room for it in the bus. We had to let it go. Standing on the side of the highway, we discussed the idea of trying to find a hospital where we could donate it to the children's wing, but it was all too much, and we just had to leave it and move on.

On a dark highway in the middle of the night, we placed my beautiful homemade dollhouse onto the shoulder, just before the grass. As we drove away, I silently cried and wiped the tears from my face as I watched it disappear from my view. My mom, trying to make me feel better, told me that some little girl would find it, love it, and take care of it, and one day, my stepfather would make me a new one. I often think about that dollhouse and wonder where it ended up and who found it. Did they love and appreciate it as I did? I really loved that dollhouse.

As we traveled through the Rocky Mountains, I sat in the back of our bus with my brother, in awe of the view. We had never seen anything so vast and beautiful. No matter what direction we looked, we saw stunning scenery. It felt like an "ooh," "ahh," and "wow" soundtrack was on a constant replay loop. As we slowly made our ascent, our stomachs filled with butterflies as we peered over the flimsy-looking guardrails.

Looking down as we puttered, as only a Volkswagen does, up the mountain, it was impossible not to realize how small we were and how magnificent God is to create such intricate beauty.

As we continued to climb, we went slower and slower. We all felt nervous as my mom worried about making it up the hill. Running out of gas was a common fear. It had happened before, and we knew all about the challenges it presented, but none of us wanted to consider the possibility while ascending the Rocky Mountains. We all knew the familiar sound and had felt the sudden, slow sputter that eventually gave way and halted us.

My fear set in, and I watched my mom's face to gauge the seriousness of our plight. While the sensation was the same as running out of gas, what we heard and felt wasn't caused by an empty tank. Halfway up the mountain, there was a loud, jolting bang! Startled, we all jumped a bit, then screamed as we realized our bus was rolling backward down the mountain. As it moved, we heard a loud scraping sound, and my stepfather yelled, "There's no power!"

He stepped on the gas, but nothing happened. My frantic mother screamed at us to "get out NOW!" and so we opened the sliding door and jumped. My stepfather, with his foot firmly on the brake, rolled far enough back to see scrape marks and a piece of metal in the middle of the road in front of him.

Slowly and gently moving backward as he steered the bus onto a nearby shoulder, he parked it as we all stood on the side of the road with nothing but a guardrail between us and the cliff. Getting out and assessing the situation, he discovered the engine had fallen out! Still partially connected by a few weak brackets, the weight of it dragged on the ground.

Our parents' faces were of sheer defeat as my mom asked, "What are we going to do now?" With no money and nowhere to go, we all said a prayer on the side of the road. Then, as my stepfather walked alongside the shoulder with his head hanging down, he happened to spot a wire coat hanger lying on the ground. As crazy and unbelievable as it may sound, he used that gift to affix the hanging part of the engine and miraculously got the bus running again!

Thinking back at how desperate we were and how God answered our prayers with a single, stray coat hanger was proof of His perfect timing and master plan.

A motley but grateful crew, traveling by VW bus through the Colorado Rockies

Throughout our travels, we met many people, saw tons of places, and had some incredible experiences. We picked up a few hitchhikers and even some dogs who were lost or injured on the side of the highway.

The most vivid memory I have of extra passengers involved a scene we encountered on the highway one night when a dog had darted across the road chasing a cat. The poor cat was hit by a car and already dead by the time we approached the terrible scene.

The dog had also been hit by another car but was still breathing. Jimmy, who was driving the bus at the time, saw the injured dog and immediately pulled over and began giving the dog mouth to mouth. We all stood on the side of the highway in tears as we watched helplessly. He tried his best to help him, but his injuries were too severe, and he didn't make it.

There was nothing more to do but move the dog away from the road to a better place of rest. This was when we found a second dog who, it seemed, had retreated after seeing the whole tragedy unfold. The poor dog was shaking in fear, and porcupine quills covered his mouth and snout.

We put him in the van, stopped at the next exit, and called the local police station from a payphone. Since it was the middle of the night, the local animal shelter wasn't open, so the police department recorded the incident. As travelers just passing through, the officer instructed us to call back to see if anyone reported a missing dog. My stepfather pulled the quills out with plyers, one by one, as the dog winced, and we pet him throughout the process.

After he finished, we gave the dog some food and tried to console him. He was now part of our journey and a welcome new passenger on this crazy ride. It wasn't a yellow brick road we were traveling, but it was a yellow-lined highway, and we were all searching for answers and a way home. Throughout our journey, we periodically called the police department in

Colorado to see if there were any updates or calls on a missing dog, but to no avail.

When we finally arrived in California, we were ready to plant roots and lead a more "traditional" lifestyle. We placed one last call to the Colorado police department and got word that someone had called about their dogs. "Dogs?" we said. The officer told us someone called stating their dogs had gotten out and were missing. They had been searching for a couple of weeks. When the officer gave us the descriptions, we knew we had good and bad news for their owner. We called the number and informed the owner about that late night on the highway and the other dog's fate. He was grateful for our help and drove from Colorado to California to meet us and retrieve his dog. We were sad to say goodbye, but what a happy reunion it was!

Play Track 5 (Angels or Los Angeles – Caroline Spence) in Broken Little Believer Playlist

Baggage Check:

Have you ever had to say goodbye to someone or something that you still think of or miss?

Did you ever experience being bullied? Although it may have been painful to endure at the time, do you have better clarity now as to why the bully acted the way they did?

Are you living life more compassionately because of the pain you felt, or are you angry because of it?

_____

_____

_____

_____

_____

_____

_____

_____

_____

CHAPTER 6

True Colors

Mom went back to work as a hairdresser, and Jimmy continued working construction before deciding, with Mom's support and encouragement, to go back to school and take up computer technology. Being a hairdresser in San Francisco in the 80s was an eye-opening experience. My mom's colleagues, predominantly gay men, had become good friends with her and felt a bit like an extended family to me.

The salon atmosphere was like a sorority—fun, loving, supportive, honest, and one of which I always enjoyed being part of. It reminded me of the nights I spent at the hair academy when I was younger, but better. It was eccentric and engaging. There was lots of laughter, and there were a few tears. There was always a scoop of gossip being dished out, and drama was inevitable. Every day was a fashion show, with beauty tips always in style and meant to be shared.

From the front steps of the salon, I watched my first gay pride parade. Technically, it was the International Lesbian and Gay Freedom Day Parade, and I felt like I had a front-row seat to the most exciting show ever. It was the closest thing I could imagine to Mardi Gras. The makeup, costumes, and colorful creations were not only exciting, but unlike anything I had ever seen.

From my steps above the crowd, I had a bird's eye view of the street. I could see all the posters and read the many signs held up by marchers. A beautiful feeling of warmth and connection was present in each smile and wave between the participants and me. Their mission was love, peace, and acceptance, and based on my experience through the doors just behind me, it was precisely what I had known, felt, and witnessed.

As some marched hand in hand in solidarity, others put on more of a show and solicited spectator engagement. It was high energy and filled with enthusiasm. Amidst the many expressions and examples of love, though, I felt an underlying fear and sadness, with heavy darkness hiding behind all the outwardly cheerful faces and colorful posters.

It wasn't long before the disease surfaced and made its presence known. There was a four-letter word I had overheard a few times in the salon, and it seemed that whenever it was spoken, laughter immediately ceased. AIDS was a new and growing epidemic, and many people were terrified and angry. One by one, those we knew and came to love were diagnosed with this terrible disease.

When so many people had finally found and enjoyed the freedom to be true to themselves and others, it seemed their triumphant exhale was robbed. Many citizens held their breaths as tragedy ripped through the community. To witness so many achieve liberation and experience long-awaited peace, only to feel shame, loneliness, and isolation again in such a way, was heartbreaking.

Regardless of what some might believe or how they feel about different lifestyles, I only saw human beings for whom I had developed genuine care and love. Over many months,

I watched friends deteriorate, lose weight, develop lesions, and suffer fatigue.

Beauty was woven throughout the sadness, though. Although AIDS took life from so many, I will never forget the ceaseless smiles, the perpetual prompting to add "just a little more color," and the sparkle that never dimmed in the eyes of those who wanted to love and live authentically.

I will never forget this special group of people. One person, in particular, left a profound impression on my mom and me. His name was Darryl. He was tall, good-looking, and had a great sense of style. He had long, blonde hair, and his image screamed that of a lead singer in a popular hair band. He was striking but in a quiet way. He worked alongside Mom in the salon, and they became very close. We frequently went to his apartment, where we sat, visited, had dinner, and watched as he showed us all the different ways to wear scarves, hair, and makeup.

His scarves were his trademark, kind of like Steven Tyler. He had a soft voice and a gentle soul, and although he never said anything to give me this impression, I felt he had an injured heart. I could sense that his heartache was deep, but instead of being bitter or angry, it made him more loving and sensitive. I cherished being around him. He had a peaceful and calming demeanor.

When Mom left the salon for a new job, she and Darryl kept in touch. For a time, she had trouble reaching him, and she began to worry. One day Mom called the salon after being unable to get him at home, and a short phone conversation led to tears. Before she hung up, I was afraid of what it meant. Darryl, like many of my mom's colleagues, had died of AIDS.

I think of Darryl often and remember the gentle spirit he had and the unique way he always made his friends feel loved. Thinking back at how I felt his vulnerable and injured heart, I like to believe that he is fully restored and that his heart is filled with all the love and happiness he gave—especially to us.

I recall many things from when we lived in San Francisco, but two women, in particular, made up a significant chunk of my memories. Both were neighbors I connected with in very different ways. I walked a lot as a young girl and always found myself talking to people. I was curious and unafraid.

Not long after we moved to the city, we planted roots in a corner apartment building where we lived on the top floor of our four-story apartment complex, with Dolphin, a beautiful, sleek, silky Siamese cat. From my window, I could see the opposite corner of the street where a lovely single-family home stood. An older woman who frequently tended her garden of bright flowers occupied it. She was always "put together" and wore her hair in a bun.

This neighbor seemed to delight in her routine of checking her flowers and had a tranquil presence about her. When out and about, I often smiled and said hello to her. I remember every detail of her company and the encounters I had with her, but ironically, I cannot remember her name.

We became fast friends when I was ten years old, and she was in her eighties. I spent a lot of time visiting with her, and she often had me over for tea, where she would show me her backyard garden, cats, and photos. She was an elegant, soft-spoken woman, and she fascinated me. She saw beauty and pleasure in simple things, like her tea. Although different than Memie's Canadian tea, it is still something I can smell and taste in my mind with its floral and herbal tones.

During one of our afternoon teas, I must have asked her if I could spend the night. It seems odd to me now that I was that comfortable with a woman I hadn't known that long, and even more strange that my mother felt comfortable enough to allow me to spend the night there when she had not met her.

I did spend a night at her house, and I vividly recall that simple yet grown-up adventure. There was no TV, but we had a long conversation about family, life, and the beauty of nature. When it was time for bed, she put on her nightgown, sat in front of her vanity, and slowly pulled her hair out of the bun. I was impressed at how long her hair was as she carefully brushed the long, fine, silver strands. I had never seen an older woman with such long hair and was fascinated by her gracefulness and classic beauty.

I don't know whether she had children, but she was very kind, and I enjoyed her company and stories. When we moved, that was the end of our friendship as I had no way of getting in touch with her.

We later lived in a single-family home on the other side of town, where I met another woman with whom I felt instantly connected. I walked to school, and one day, my mother asked me to take our cat, Dolphin, to the vet on my way. As I walked with my backpack and a pet carrier, I happened to pass a middle-aged woman walking in the same direction but at a slower pace.

I smiled and said "hello," and she inquired about my cat. She picked up her pace a bit, and I slowed slightly so that we were soon walking together and chatting about my plans to drop my cat off at the vet on my way to school.

My usual walk to school seemed longer than expected as we talked about everything and learned so much about one another in this short time. The woman, Candi, lived just a block over from us, was divorced, and had a son a year or two older than me. She also had cancer. I told her that my mother had had cancer and that they should meet. Candi remarked how mature I was for my age and said she would love to talk with Mom.

Later that day, I excitedly told my mom about my morning encounter and told her that I wanted her to meet Candi. My mother was much less excited than I was and quickly said that she didn't want to talk about her illness or revisit it. It took some prompting for her to agree to meet, but Mom, Candi, and I finally got together at my new friend's house.

This connection was a bit strange for me at first because I felt closer to Candi than my mom did. Still, after being introduced to Candi's son and encouraged to get to know him better while the moms spent time chatting in the kitchen, my mom and Candi seemed to find their stride, and a friendship eventually evolved. Candi's son and I didn't immediately hit it off; it was a bit awkward, but we found similarities in our music and fashion taste.

We went to an amusement park together, where we delved into deeper conversations about our mothers' health. I had already lived through the fear of cancer and seen the ugly side of it. I was fortunate that my mother survived it, although I continued to worry. He was alone and scared. He feared for his mother, and I could tell. Candi loved the sun and, ultimately, her desire and the pleasure she derived from sitting outside in the backyard and soaking in the rays was her choice and the way she would inevitably die.

"I want my MTV" is a song that always brings me back to the days of hanging out with another young person who would live and learn the sadness and cruelty of loss.

*Play Track 6 (True Colors – Cyndi Lauper) in Broken Little
Believer Playlist*

Baggage Check:

Have you ever met someone and instantly felt a connection?
Do you find yourself still thinking about this person regardless
of how much time has passed?

_____

_____

_____

_____

_____

_____

_____

_____

_____

_____

_____

_____

CHAPTER 7

Testify

From the beginning of my mother's marriage to my stepfather, things were never really "normal." What should have been a celebratory honeymoon turned into a fight for her life. Trials and tribulations replaced their anticipated newlywed bliss. My mom had endured a lot. Besides the bone marrow transplant, she underwent full-body radiation and chemo, and now, was unable to have any more children. Her infertility bothered her deeply because she knew Jimmy wanted a child of his own, and she wanted one with him.

They had looked forward to this when marrying. While Mom was still grateful for a second chance at life, she couldn't help but take inventory of the many changes her body went through and how they left her feeling like less of a woman. She complained that her hair and skin weren't the same and her body was different. The after-effects of treatment haunted her, and she grew frustrated at the price she still paid.

It bothered her that she was already a few years older than Jimmy, and now she was dealing with low self-esteem and insecurity. She grew suspicious of my stepfather, and if he was late coming home from work, she questioned him incessantly, accusing him of cheating. Whether he was then or not, I don't know, but she was concerned.

Her unease continued for a while, and I believe it was the wedge that began to separate them. They argued a lot, and when he would go out with his friends and new connections he made in computer classes, she would wake me up in the middle of the night and say that I needed to come with her to look for him.

We drove up and down streets where Jimmy's friends lived until she spotted his car. She would park at the end of the block and instruct me to sneak down to the house and peek in the window and try to see him. He grew tired of being accused, and ultimately, her suspicions became a reality. My mother never hesitated to say how she felt or what she thought, which included her feelings about men. The consistent message I heard was that "men are all liars and cheaters, and you can never trust them." I grew up seeing and believing this.

We had always been part of the Catholic Church, but we attended a non-denominational, Bible-based missionary church when we arrived in California. I don't recall who invited us; it could have been a neighbor, a colleague of my moms, or a complete stranger for all I know, but I do remember that my mom was intrigued, a bit desperate, and in need of hope, so we all went one Sunday.

Everyone greeted us warmly and welcomed us with open arms. Friendly, kind, and full of compassion, this church and its members were bursting with love and energy. It reminded me of that little church I went to in Nebraska. As the service began, having predominantly Catholic mass as my frame of reference, I couldn't help but notice and appreciate some stark differences. The music was less traditional, and the parishioners were lively and engaged. Some people danced, some sang, and others called out to the Lord. I would later discover that this type of church fell into the evangelistic category, which intrigued me.

At one of these services, while everyone was singing loud, praising the Lord, and speaking in tongues, the minister invited anyone who wanted a closer relationship with God to come to the front. With great passion, he spoke in a rich and inviting tone, saying, "If you feel a calling, a knocking on your heart, now is the time to answer it. Come forward and accept the invitation."

I wanted a closer relationship with God! I wondered to myself if I heard knocking or felt a calling. I watched as people stepped out of their pews and filled the center aisle to make their way to the front of the church. As I sat there, feeling like a nervous yet curious onlooker, I witnessed hands being laid on people as they cried out dramatically.

I tried to keep my head down in prayer, but I was enthralled with what was happening and found myself fixed on this unfamiliar and captivating experience. A woman seated next to me slowly raised her arms and, with her hands outstretched in the air, repeated, "Jesus, come to us." As she rocked back and forth, she continued calling out and then gently grabbed my hand and raised it with hers.

"Join in, child. Go on," she prompted as she repeated invitations for the Lord to draw near. Hesitantly and somewhat embarrassed, I began to repeat after her as she nodded in approval. The parishioner grabbed my arm and led me to the front of the sanctuary, where we kneeled together at the altar. She continued to hold my hand and raise it high in the air. I never looked back at my mom, so I don't know what she was thinking or doing, but as the music and singing continued, my companion called out to the Lord as she clutched my hand in hers and said, "Come, Lord Jesus. Come."

I didn't know what was happening at first, but this day I felt the spirit of Christ move through me. I physically felt a surge of love and energy swoosh through me, and I surprised myself, crying as I never had before—nor have I since. They were tears of joy. The kind of tears that make you ask yourself why you are sobbing when you feel so happy. I have never felt anything so beautiful in all my life. It wasn't of this world. It wasn't an emotion or feeling that I can even explain; it was a sacred moment.

I had always felt a relationship with God, but I had never experienced anything like I did that day. I felt Jesus and His presence move through me. On this occasion, I was born again. When the minister asked if I wanted to invite Jesus into my life and heart, I knew He had already arrived, but I answered with an emphatic, "yes."

We continued to attend this church, and we became more and more involved. It was an active congregation, and there were always activities going on, especially for the younger generations. I learned here that a parish's health could be determined by its number of active young people.

We youth were encouraged to get involved. It was easy to join in with a variety of groups and events to choose from and participate in. The youth music group recruited me, and it was a natural fit. I had always enjoyed singing, and music was a passion that had sustained me in many ways through-out my life. I met other kids but soon discovered that I was one of the younger ones in the group. It wasn't long before I realized that this wasn't your typical church choir. They were energetic, charismatic, and devoted singers. They enthusiasti-cally welcomed me, and I quickly learned many of their songs.

They weren't only Christian songs, but music they wrote, rehearsed, and recorded. I enjoyed singing with this group and found that I always felt uplifted after rehearsals and performances. What I didn't realize, however, was that my recruitment and ongoing involvement was for discipleship—PUBLIC discipleship! We went out in vans to sing and witness to people walking and passing by on the streets.

We were the young missionaries, and we sang on street corners, in office lobbies, and even in restaurants if permitted. I learned that it was part of our mission as Christians to help spread the message. "We must speak God's word and share His message. That is what we are called to do." I was uncomfortable and embarrassed the first few times I went out, especially when other kids my age would pass by and stare, but soon it became second nature and enjoyable.

While singing, I experienced that same feeling I had when I went caroling in that little Nebraska town. There was a warm joy that filled my body as I sang with all my heart. I no longer saw the eyes of curiosity or disbelief but connected with the eyes who needed to hear our message through music. I understood what being a missionary was all about and the power of the testimonies we shared.

One day, while out on one of our paths, the youth minister told us to start making our way toward a nearby restaurant. He went ahead of us and asked us to wait in the entrance area when we got there. I thought we were stopping for lunch and that he was going ahead of us to get a table for the group. It was a day I will never forget. As I stood in the entryway, I overheard our youth minister ask the owner if he would consider feeding us in exchange for entertaining his guests.

What? I thought, frozen in place. The idea of singing for food was mortifying and humiliating, but the church firmly taught and lived by the belief that God always provides for those who trust in Him. This request was faith in action. As humble servants of God, there was no reason to worry about where our next meal would come from, we only needed to glorify and trust in Him, and he would make a way.

On that day, and the days that followed, He did just that. It wasn't always comfortable, and at times I feared the outcome, but God always provided, and we never went hungry. Singing to a restaurant filled with people in exchange for a bowl of soup and a piece of bread was something I will never forget.

As a young girl, it was a humbling yet spiritually awakening experience that I carry with me to this day. It was this type of missionary discipleship and witnessing to others that changed me for the better. I became vulnerable in the most beautiful way and experienced what it meant to fully trust in Him, to rely on my faith, and to listen to my inner voice. Any selfish pride that may have resided in me was washed away in that moment, and my soul was cleansed in a way I could never describe in words. A simple bowl of soup and a slice of bread never tasted so good and nourished me both physically and spiritually.

The church believed that to trust God, one must relinquish worldly possessions and donate them to the church. The idea was that everyone within the church community shared their gifts and talents to benefit the faith family, and together, trust that God will provide the rest. Committing to help one another by sharing our strengths, skills, and possessions included donating our vehicles, as others had done, for the good of the church and its members. We were called to be a family of God.

It was a simple way of life that opened my eyes to a different world. Adapting to this communal way of living was initially strange, but with increasing involvement, it became routine. Growing connections, reassuring messages, and the call to missionary service led us to a time when we found it difficult to imagine life before joining the church.

Many of the songs that I grew up listening to and singing at this church were prophetic in nature. They were stories within songs, and my young and impressionable mind was opened and altered as my spirit was deeply moved listening to them. Some brought about fear but most stirred comfort in my heart as it related to faith. They were songs intended for children, but the themes and messages were mature and ranged from divorce to greed, death, and the devil's temptations lurking in technology.

In the eighties, when personal technology was only beginning, we sang songs that foretold a future where we would be microchipped and brainwashed by the devil. Our thoughts would be infiltrated with the lure of convenience. With a refrain, "Watch out for 666 and his computer tricks,"[3] the idea of men becoming like robots was planted, and I grew up believing technology would come at a price and freedom would inevitably be compromised. This song was so powerful that as I grew older and technology became more advanced, I felt that I was witnessing this melodic prophecy unfold before my eyes.

Another song began with a family having a conversation in their car after the husband picked up his wife from the airport one rainy night. A little girl's voice is heard welcoming her mom home from her trip as she gets in the car. Moments later, you hear the mom screaming to her husband, "Watch out!" just before loud, screeching noises and a final fiery bang as the windshield wipers slosh back and forth in the background.

As the song begins, you hear the little girl calling out for her family as they all make their way to Heaven. The dialogue describes what they see and feel along the way when they realize they are dead. This song elicited many emotions within me: shock, fear, worry, and then, as the song's beat picked up, feelings of peace, comfort, and reassurance.

These songs certainly got my attention as a little girl, and their messages stayed with me forever. They added to my already heightened awareness of life's uncertainties and future unknowns. I looked at things differently because of these songs. Even though I already knew life could change instantly, the radical teachings and powerful lessons the church taught left me with a deeper, more contemplative approach to life.

Ultimately, my mom decided she wanted more for her life and her children. She was tired of living unpredictably and didn't want to rely on anyone else. She had a devout faith and believed she could live a good life without having to give up everything they worked so hard to regain. Giving up her vehicle was probably the deciding factor. Having to depend on a community for basic transportation was not her idea of freedom. Ironically, we nicknamed our VW bus "Freedom" as it carried us through hard times and delivered us from heartache. My mother was never a conformist; she has too loud a voice to sit quietly and do as she's told. It was time to rebuild our lives, and she prepared to do so the same way she always had, by working hard and trusting God to guide and protect us.

Bernadette and Jimmy started with a clean slate and decided to renew their vows on the top of a mountain in beautiful California. But ultimately, all the effort in the world and changes in scenery wouldn't save them. My mom's marriage to Jimmy failed, and they went their separate ways. She always said that the used wedding dress she wore from Goodwill was bad luck.

I can't help but think of their wedding song and find beautiful and prophetic meaning in the words, "For whenever two or more of you are gathered in His name, there is love. There is love." There was love—a lot of it. "Is it love that brings you here, or is love that brings you life?" I believe that love is what brought them there, and it was love that gave her life.

For years, I would hear all about how she helped make his life better. He was "just a construction worker" when they met, and now he had a successful career in computers after she made sacrifices for him to go back to school. I knew why my mom was bitter. Why wouldn't she be? She was divorced again, a single mom of two, and had overcome a horrific illness that left her resentful and worried about her future health. Life was hard, and it didn't seem fair. I tried to look at things differently, though. I believed she and my stepfather helped make each other's lives better.

It wasn't the union they'd dreamed it would be, but my mother wasn't alone. She had him by her side when she was sick and not expected to survive. She could cry, scream, and yell with or at him. She had a traveling companion who worked to put gas in the bus and get us from point A to point Z, and the adventures that took place between all of those points created a fantastic story. It wasn't a fancy life, but it was a part I look back on and smile because we were together. In times of chaos, we found solace and comfort in each other. It was the original version of the TV series, *Survivor*, but this reality, as dysfunctional as it might have been, was mine.

Play Track 7 (Testify – Need to Breathe) in Broken Little Believer Playlist

Baggage Check:

Have you ever faced a radical change in your life? Were you resistant to it, or did you welcome it? Can you look back on that change now and find purpose and reason for it?

_____

_____

_____

_____

_____

_____

_____

_____

_____

_____

_____

_____

CHAPTER 8

Underdog

We made our way back to New York, and once again, we were a family of three. We lived in a small duplex apartment on a dead-end street. As animal lovers, we always wanted a pet, but we didn't have the time or money for one. That didn't stop animals from finding us, though.

My brother happened to find a stray dog one day, and he followed Chris home. He was so cute and so affectionate. We begged my mom to let us keep him, and she gave us a few days to try and find the owner or a home for him. When the days were up, she felt we couldn't take on another responsibility or expense. We were heartbroken, but he never left. Despite not being allowed in, he remained outside and continued to hang around our house.

Opposite his temperament, my brother named him Cujo, like the movie. I never saw it, but I knew our Cujo was nothing like that dog. Cujo never wanted to be away from us. He would follow us to school every day and sit outside until school was dismissed, then walked home with us. If we left the house by car, Cujo would run down the middle of the street after us. Even though he wasn't "our" dog, he claimed us, and Chris and I loved him.

Mom pulled over many times, fearing Cujo would get hit by a car. We'd take him back to our house, command him to "stay," only to spot him in the rearview mirror chasing after us again. My brother and I would gasp and screech as we witnessed him nearly be hit by cars as he desperately tried to catch us. It was heartbreaking, and we cried a lot. In his eyes, I felt him saying, "Please don't leave me," as we would beg my mom to stop.

It eventually became too much with all she was already doing, and she couldn't be responsible for a dog. One day, animal control picked him up outside our school, and they asked Mom if he belonged to us. She said no, so they took him. My brother and I cried and cried because we knew how much he loved us, and we only wanted him to know how much we loved him. Abandonment is a feeling I know and understand well.

I didn't own some of the basics many kids took for granted, let alone wear the latest fashions they donned. In middle school, I gravitated to friends on the outskirts of the popular scene—not because that's where my clothes and socioeconomic label placed me, but because I felt most comfortable being there. I had nothing in common with the "in" kids. If I had a more expensive wardrobe, that would have been the extent of our superficial similarities.

I wasn't concerned about trivial things, like what color Converse shoes were hot that week, what boy was the cutest according to the girls, whose family had the most money, best car, or the coolest jobs. I had experienced a different life and never felt comfortable with people who didn't seem "real" or honest. It didn't help matters that I witnessed a lot of meanness in popular groups, and I despised that type of behavior.

I was out walking in my neighborhood one sunny day, and just a few short blocks from my house, I noticed a girl hanging out in her backyard. She was sitting on top of a picnic table, listening to Richard Marks on her portable stereo. For whatever reason, I decided to walk up to her and introduce myself. We became fast friends, which seemed meant to be as we happened to be in the same grade. Claire lived with her grandmother, and we spent many afternoons together hanging out, going to the mall, planning sleepovers, and replaying that Richard Marks cassette tape over and over again.

Claire's parents were divorced, and her mother remarried. Although she had a good relationship with her mom, living with her grandmother worked for everyone. In some ways, we had a lot in common. We were both very close to our grandmothers, had untraditional families, lived near one another, and shared many of the same interests.

However, we were also very different. Claire valued brand names. I didn't dispute their quality, but I shopped at Joyce Leslie because I knew I would get more for my money. Claire had a crush on the most popular boy in school, who would secretly visit her but publicly deny any relationship. On the other hand, I had a crush on a boy who was not just cute but sweet, kind, and unashamed to say hi to me in school.

I learned valuable lessons in middle school. One was on a day we had a substitute teacher in English. My best friend, Claire, who happened to be in the same class, sat several rows away from me. Living in a predominantly well-to-do area, I knew that many girls were mean and catty and loved to gang up on the weak.

I never understood the motivation behind picking on someone just because you could, but when a group of young, rich, popular girls got together, things often happened that I didn't understand. I had no interest in their group and paid no attention to them. But Claire wanted to fit in and having more financial resources than I did, she straddled the "popular" fence with her name-brand clothes.

There was a widely used acronym back then to describe a girl who came from money and embraced the title and lifestyle of a princess. While it may be offensive today, the girls I went to school with were proud of the classification and self-identified as such. During English, one of the "in" girls started making fun of what I was wearing.

I remember it as if it was yesterday. I had thought it was one of my best Goodwill purchases! I loved my brand name yellow pants and the fashionable red shirt. I didn't consider or connect to the familiar color combination, but she did and proceeded to call me Ronald McDonald. It didn't take long for her friends to join in the fun and laugh as they picked apart my outfit. One of the girls yelled from across the room, "Ooh, nice outfit! Where'd you get it? Kmart? Goodwill?" It was hilarious (for them), especially since they unknowingly guessed correctly.

As they continued to taunt and tease, the laughter grew, and my friend sat silently. At one point, I casually called out her name, saying, "Hey, Claire!" hoping to either prompt a distraction, sequester a little support, or just change the subject, but she quickly turned away, put her head down, and acted like she didn't know me. She was my best friend. Of course, her shun hurt me, and I felt betrayed.

When our teacher returned, she began class by announcing how disappointed she was in everyone's behavior while a substitute was covering for her. She started by sharing that the report she received from the teacher indicated that students were misbehaving and picking on a classmate while she was out. As she continued, I sank lower and lower in my chair in embarrassment and fear that her reprimand would only bring more unwanted attention to me.

When she finished with her vague yet painfully revealing announcement, she proceeded to assign every student in the class the task of writing me an apology letter. As if I wasn't humiliated enough! Ironically, my best friend was exempt from this punitive assignment because we were known to be close friends, and surely, she must not have been involved.

Little did my teacher know, her apology was the only one I needed or wanted. Although she never acknowledged that day and all that had transpired, I let it go and, we continued being friends as though nothing had ever happened. I knew what it felt like to be forsaken, and the pain served to deepen my sense of loyalty to others. I would not remain silent or look the other way if I observed someone being bullied, taken advantage of, or mistreated. As for my friend, I don't know that she ever felt any remorse, nor have I ever asked her, but I certainly learned a valuable lesson that day. I believe the pain that stemmed from it made me a more empathetic, protective friend.

Play Track 8 (Underdog – Alicia Keys) in Broken Little Believer Playlist

Baggage Check:

Have you ever experienced betrayal? Can you remember how it felt? How did it change you? Or is there baggage that you still need to relinquish?

_____

_____

_____

_____

_____

_____

_____

_____

_____

_____

_____

_____

_____

CHAPTER 9

Because of You

I noticed a marked difference in my mom after moving back to the East Coast. Her once easy-going, flexible temperament had turned rigid, angry, and filled with resentment. She felt cheated, and her bitterness over how her life had turned out trickled down to me. Mom had set the stage for communicating through uncensored discussion long ago, but now that I was older, her unedited words were harsh, dirty, and carried more of a punch.

Like many pre-pubescent girls, I went through an awkward period, and I was already very self-conscious. With a recycled wardrobe, I learned how to be creative with my outfits and tried, sometimes successfully, to set new trends. What I couldn't be creative with, though, was my hair.

I was often my mom's hair model in the salon and given hairstyles that were better suited for braver souls. Looking in the mirror, I saw all that was wrong with me. I didn't like my hair, and my large, overcrowded teeth that filled my mouth were beginning to overlap in the front. Mom said I could fix my smile if I applied pressure with my thumb to them consistently. I was flat-chested, the last girl in her class to get her period, and I certainly didn't come from money or a conventional, intact family.

As my grandmother tried to explain to me, my mom saw me as a budding young woman (no pun intended), and my reflection proved to be a painful one to her as well, but for different reasons. According to my grandmother, I was a reminder of Bernadette's lost opportunities, youth, and in some way, freedom. Mom struggled with her own feelings of bitterness, loss, and regret.

I didn't understand why my own mother insulted me, put me down, mimicked me, and was impossible to please. I only tried to make things easier for her. As a single mother, the expectation was that I would clean the house, help cook, and watch Chris. I was always a pleaser, but it became an unhealthy challenge when I would race around the house and try to make things perfect to surprise her before she came home.

I would stand by the door when I heard her car pull in the driveway and excitedly wait for her to walk into the house. With great anticipation, I would say, "So, what do you think?" as I revealed the clean house in a Vanna White arm gesture manner. Her response of "What do you want me to do, jump up and down?" would crush me.

It seemed nothing was ever good enough for her. I worked hard to get good grades, and when a teacher would send her a positive note about me, she said that good grades, cleaning the house, and other duties were expected; there were no awards or recognition for that. While it was a harsh lesson back then, it shaped who I am today. It was my grandmother, Memie, who told me Mom was jealous. It wasn't until much later in life that I realized pleasing her was not my job or responsibility.

Despite her fits of anger, I loved my mom and felt sad watching her work hard and struggle to make ends meet. As a result, I tried my best to do whatever I could to make things easier for her.

During these tumultuous middle school years, I struggled with confidence and self-esteem and likely appeared timid to others. Although I had been recognized for good grades and had received several academic awards, I was always at the edge of my seat and never entirely at ease. Whenever I found a "comfortable" position or stride, it seemed my mom thought the best way to keep me humble and appreciative was to knock me down a notch or two. Consequently, I found that keeping my head down and quietly trying to blend in was the best way to get through these years.

My middle school principal was a tall, serious-looking man who knew my name and used it regularly as he asked me how I was doing or how my day was. At that time in my life, any form of attention was something that left me feeling uncomfortable. My perception of myself, a combination of what others had told me and what I saw in the mirror, wasn't great and left me uneasy.

As I walked through the halls at school with a strong persona but unsure interior, he was a consistent, smiling source of generous support and encouragement. Having gotten to be more familiar with him because of my good grades and various honor roll achievements, I began to appreciate his check-ins and looked forward to our chats.

Mature beyond my years, conversations with adults came naturally. He didn't just ask me how my day was for the sake of asking. I came to find that he sincerely and genuinely wanted to know. On occasion, we would have lunch together in his office, and we would talk about school, life, family, and friends. Most importantly, he would ask me about my dreams, hopes, and wishes for the future. He got me into the habit of thinking about these things and considering what I envisioned for my life. He must have seen something in me or knew I needed emotional support.

Although he noticed every student and tried to bring out the best in everyone, his astuteness and relentless mission to want to make me believe in myself changed these years for me and proved to be a pivotal experience.

It was years before my mom began to date again, and when she met a seemingly decent guy who was a hard worker, the bonus was that he didn't run when she told him that she had two kids. They got along well, both owned businesses, and they shared a lot of the same interests, but there were some oddities about their relationship as well. Regardless, it was a relief to see my mom happy again.

I noticed that my mom would always tell me to go to my room whenever he came over. I assumed it was to allow them some time alone but realized the same rule didn't apply to my brother. I never understood why she always sent me upstairs when he came over. My initial assumption changed when one night, I happened to go downstairs to get something from the kitchen and had to pass through the living room to get there.

They were sitting on the couch, talking, and she proceeded to get up and follow me in the kitchen to ask me what I was doing. Wearing Bermuda shorts, I stood in the kitchen utterly unprepared for the poison that would seep out of her tight lips but that her eyes braced me for.

Whispering so that he wouldn't hear, she proceeded to ask me if I was trying to turn her boyfriend on. Sick to my stomach by the insinuation, I went back to my room feeling disgusted, embarrassed, and ashamed. I was so upset by the thought of it, and the fact that she would even imply such a thing led me to not only stay in my room or go to my friend's house as often as I could but to look away quickly anytime he was in my presence.

We went up to Memie and Boppie's as often as we could. I loved being there and enjoyed spending time with my grandparents. The holidays were always special, and the whole family, aunts, uncles, and cousins would gather in their small but warm, cozy, and inviting home on the reservoir. In warm weather, I was out and about exploring the woods and walking on the many trails. In the winter, there was sledding, ice skating, and lots of family time sitting around the wood-burning stove where Memie always had a kettle that gave off aromatic scents that filled the house. I could never be bored at Memie and Boppie's. There was always something to do or see.

The winters made things even more interesting, and the adventure trying to make it up their steep hill in the snow was a test we excitedly attempted. The only way to determine if it was possible was to start driving up. When the snow got too high or the road was too icy or slippery, inevitably, we would begin to slide backward, trying to avoid ending up in the ditch. There were two ways to get up the mountain, but we always attempted the steep way first because it was shorter. If we couldn't make it up that way, we'd have to go the long way around. No matter which route we took, the top of the mountain was where we needed and wanted to be.

From a young age, I took notice of things and would pick up on emotional undercurrents. Family gatherings were no exception. It seemed no matter what, an unpleasant exchange would ensue, and somehow, my mom was typically involved. I'm not saying she was to blame or the cause of all of the arguments, but she always found her way into the mix. Inevitably, it would turn into a "That's it! We're leaving. Let's go!" announcement from my mom.

I always hated how we left. It was usually in the middle of something fun, just before dessert was served, or just as presents were to be opened. Mom was stubborn, and when she said something or made up her mind, there was no turning back. That was a sign of weakness, and her independent, Irish heritage wouldn't have it. Mom made us get into the car and drive home prematurely on many occasions because she was upset over something that someone said or did.

The incessant, unresolved matters, hasty departures, hanging up of phones, or walking away from people always bothered me deeply and left me wanting to bridge the communication gap. It created within me a desire to never leave things unsaid or allow words to be misconstrued. It taught me to observe people, their body language, and tone of voice while closely listening to their stories. It made me sensitive to energy and swift, volatile behavior changes. It became my challenge always to want to help overcome and resolve problems for others. I witnessed so much miscommunication and blown opportunities for forgiveness and understanding that I couldn't help but feel sad and helpless.

The summer before I started high school, my mom instructed me to pack some clothes because we were going to visit my grandparents for the weekend. There was nothing unusual about this, and like every other time, I was excited to go. After the three-and-a-half-hour drive, Mom pulled up to their house and told me to grab my bag and head in while she parked the car. I rushed in, hugged my grandparents, and put my bag down. Something in my grandmother's face told me that all wasn't right.

From the corner of my eye, I caught a glimpse of Mom's car facing the opposite direction. She never came in, and I stood there watching her drive away as a cloud of country dust followed her car down the dirt road. I was shocked, angry, and sad. Not because I was at my grandparents, but because my mother lied to me. Why?

My grandmother confessed that she disagreed with my mother's plan and knew that what my mom had told her wasn't true. My mom told Memie that I was getting out of control, and she wanted to leave me there for the summer to teach me a lesson.

I was furious with my mom for doing that to me. I felt no different from all the animals dumped and left behind that my grandmother took in and cared for. I had made plans with my friends for the summer and had even tried out and made the High School Color Guard team. In a time before cell phones and email, I worried about how I was going to tell my friends and my coach what happened and why I wasn't there.

I was angry and humiliated, and I didn't understand any of it! I got good grades, never went to parties or got in trouble, had a small group of good, quiet friends, and never talked back to my mom. Anything that came even remotely close to sass would get me slapped or my hair pulled, so I was very cautious around my mom. This "sentence" that she imposed upon me didn't make sense, and I was mad.

Once I got over the shock of being dumped, I set out to make the best of my time upstate and welcomed the long, slower-paced summer days. I fished, swam, rowed the boat, and hiked in the woods. Fascinated by all things in nature, I dug for worms, studied tadpoles, witnessed the laying and hatching of eggs, observed animals being born, and watched wildflowers come to life.

When I wasn't outdoors, I spent my time playing cards and Scrabble with my grandmother and sharing cups of tea. We made countless trips to town, where she would run errands that always took longer than planned because we would bump into someone she knew, and lengthy conversations ensued.

The county fair was going on, and my grandmother offered to take me. As we stood in line to buy tickets, I begged my grandmother to get the wristband so that I could go on unlimited rides. Of course, it was more expensive for the wristband, but if I were sure I would use it, she would buy it. Excitedly, I told her all about the many rides I planned to go on. After eating a hot dog and then going on the tilt a whirl, however, the wristband didn't get much use. I always felt sorry about that, but luckily, she felt worse for me and my stomach than she did about the lost money.

While we were walking around the fairgrounds, a tall, blonde woman approached us and said, "Shanie? Oh, my goodness, you've gotten so big!" Having no idea who she was, my grandmother made the introduction and informed me that she was my aunt on my father's side.

In such a large family with many relatives I didn't know, including so many of their offspring, I quickly learned the chances were fairly high that any tall blonde in that area could very well be a relative of mine from that side. Speaking to my newly introduced aunt, a mixture of fascination, curiosity, and awkward small talk followed on my end before I attempted a few more *mild* rides to get the most out of my grandmother's investment.

With the windows rolled down and a soft summer breeze blowing in, my grandmother drove us home. Along the way, she shared tidbits about my father's side of the family and named my aunts and uncles who lived in the area. It was intriguing to hear more about the family I never knew.

In the middle bedroom at my grandparents' home hung an illuminated, plug-in portrait of Jesus kneeling by a large rock with His hands folded in prayer. As He looked up to the skies, beams of light shone down from Heaven and warmly covered His face. This image was the last thing I saw before going to bed each night and the first thing I saw each morning. I loved this picture and found comfort in the light and the peaceful, hopeful expression Jesus had upon His face as he looked up toward the sky. This image made me feel safe and reminded me of Jesus' faithfulness in his Father and how I could put my faith in Him.

After the fair, I woke up in the middle of the night and felt like I would be sick. My grandmother must have turned the illuminated picture off, and although I knew that room well, I was disoriented and couldn't find the door. I felt the bed and intuitively reached for the walls in search of the doorknob so that I could get to the bathroom, but without the light, I couldn't see anything. I went around and around the tiny room, feeling the walls, desperately trying to hold down my vomit while I searched for the way out.

I called out to my grandmother, but she didn't hear me. It was a terrifying feeling not being able to get out of a room I knew so well. I couldn't hold the sickness down any longer and threw up on the bedroom floor and went back to bed. The light that shined behind Jesus as He kneeled and prayed at the rock represented much more to me now. I knew He was my light, my direction, and my hope as He continued to guide me onto the path meant for me. Without Him, I felt lost and in the dark in every sense.

A few days after the county fair, my grandmother yelled out, "Shanie…telephone." On the other end was a deep but soft-spoken voice that slowly and hesitantly asked, "How have you been?" Confused, I asked, "Who is this?" As I stood in front of the rotary phone hanging on the wall, everything seemed to stop moving except for the long, dangling cord that tethered the receiver to the base.

"It's your dad," he said before quickly jumping into telling me how sorry he was for not being there for me and how he regretted not trying harder to be involved in my life after we left all those years ago.

With a cord long enough to stretch from the kitchen to the living room, I walked over to the couch, sat down, and listened. My dad said all the things I wanted to hear as a young girl, and it probably sounded sweeter after all that had happened with my mom. No stranger to feelings of abandonment, his words were redeeming in some way.

After he let it all out, as if my father knew he had to speak fast to avoid being hung up on, he asked if I would mind a visit. After a long, perplexed pause and not knowing how to respond, I said, "Sure. I guess so."

He and his current wife drove from Nebraska to New York in her little red sports car and spent a week visiting his many family members who still lived there and me. They took me out for dinner, bought me a couple of outfits, and we walked downtown. As we passed a jewelry store, I awkwardly stared at a jewelry case because I didn't know how to fill the empty, silent moments. My father asked me if I liked a particular necklace. Not sure which one he was referring to, I said "yes" only to be polite, not knowing he would go in and buy it for me.

It was a pretty but simple silver woven chain that made a hard V at the neckline. I had never had a piece of jewelry before, besides cheap, assorted, stud earrings, so while it wasn't something I would have picked out myself or ever asked for, I felt important wearing it.

At the end of the week, my father presented a shocking question, asking if I would like to drive back out to Nebraska with them and see where they lived. He described their home and the town they lived in, saying that it was much nicer than the place we stayed at when I was younger. He urged me to think it over and was adamant that I would like it. It was nice to be wanted.

My mother was furious, and again, angry with my grandparents, although they played no part in this and could not have predicted that we would run into Scott's sister at the fair, that she would call him, or that any of this would happen. My mom was quick to give me an ultimatum, saying that I would never be allowed to step foot in her house again if I went. I was hurt, torn, and afraid, but I also knew what I would be going back to at my mom's and secretly hoped things would be different this time with my dad.

Play Track 9 (Because Of You – Kelly Clarkson) in Broken Little Believer Playlist

Baggage Check:

Do you carry any baggage that is not yours? Have you taken on expectations of others that are heavy and do not belong to you?

_____

_____

_____

_____

_____

_____

_____

_____

_____

_____

_____

_____

CHAPTER 10

Like A Rock

The car ride to Nebraska was cramped. I sat in the middle of the back seat of the tiny sports car with my knees in my chest, but I was more anxious about where I was going than how I was getting there. As he drove, my father's wife Mandy told me stories about her family, the town they lived in, and things that I might enjoy doing and seeing.

I could tell she wanted me to feel comfortable, and when she asked me about my interests, hobbies, and dreams, I felt special. Mandy played a lot of music and frequently asked me if I knew the song that was playing and if I liked it. She played a lot of Bob Seger, and I liked it.

I will never forget when the song, *Like A Rock*, came on, and she turned around and said, "This song reminds me of you, Shane." I had always liked that song, but after she made that announcement to me, I listened to every single word with such intent in hopes of getting a glimpse of what she saw in me. It was one of the best compliments I had received until that point in my life, and it inspired me to continue being strong.

I didn't necessarily feel strong like a rock, but I had conviction, and I was ready to take on the world and all the changes in store for me. I was prepared to explore this new direction. I knew I had to escape the inevitable and foreseeable roadblocks and try a new path. Nebraska—so foreign, yet exciting, with open skies and clear roads, it proved to be the medicine I needed. Tackling more lessons and finding additional uncertainties were part of everyday life for me. Still, the sweet, unexpected moments and the people I met and came to know became the family every teenage girl needed.

When we first arrived, I felt like a celebrity. My father paraded me around town and was eager to show me off as his daughter. People were different here. The energy felt unpretentious, and the people, warm and welcoming. It was a bigger town for Nebraska but tiny for someone coming from New York.

I made friends quickly and easily and loved the feel of a small town. I acclimated readily and found the wide-open spaces and big, uninterrupted skies to be good for my soul. Mandy taught me how to make sun tea and cabbage burgers and how to achieve a perfectly golden tan in the backyard. She was tough, firm, but fair. There was no sleeping in on Saturdays. Saturday was chore day, and she expected me to help. Even though I may have groaned a bit when the sound of the vacuum and loud music woke me early Saturday mornings, she was the one who maintained order, taught responsibility, and expected me to follow the rules.

All this order and expectation contributed to the sense of respect that I was accustomed to and knew children should have. Mandy was a beautiful, thin blonde who loved Newport News and ordered clothing from their catalog often. She would let me borrow a shirt on occasion (one I even wore in my freshman yearbook picture), but I'm getting ahead of myself.

I fell in love with this tiny town, and it felt like I was home. When my father and Mandy extended the invitation to stay in Nebraska and be enrolled in school, I didn't hesitate. I was instantly popular, and it was easy getting to know everyone. With popularity came responsibility, and I believed that part of that responsibility was to be kind to everyone. As a result, I was part of many circles. I hung out with the jocks, nerds, ranchers, farmers, stoners, and those who struggled to find their place.

Unfortunately, it wouldn't be long before my father's marriage began to crumble. My stepmother, who felt compelled to reassure me that it had nothing to do with me, said quite simply, "I just don't love him anymore." When the moment of truth arrived, and they discussed things behind closed doors, I overheard him pleading with her as he suggested that he would send me back to New York if that would make things better.

"How dare you!" Mandy asserted as she expressed her disgust in my father's quick willingness to get rid of me. I will never forget those words or that day. It was the day when everything changed.

Shortly after she moved out, I began to see the man I remembered from years ago. He was depressed, moped around the house, and didn't speak to me unless I initiated it. He went out all the time, came home drunk, and often with different women night after night. There were never any "good mornings." If we awoke at the same time, we passed each other in the kitchen. The only sounds that broke up the silence were pouring coffee and the rattling daily paper.

I was free to come and go as I pleased. It didn't matter my age. My friends all envied me and thought my dad was "so cool." Meanwhile, I craved the affection, protection, and stability of a responsible parent. While I had the freedom to do whatever I wanted, I also had a solid moral compass driven into me and knew that if my friends with responsible, loving parents weren't out, I shouldn't be either. Plus, who would I be hanging out with if they were all home?

I never knew what I might discover in the mornings. One day, a hung-over woman tried to strike up a conversation with me as I got ready for school. Another day, I didn't see anyone but heard that Scott had a guest. I just went about my business. This existence with my father went on for almost a year as I focused on school, maintained my grades, and even collected several academic and performance awards.

Despite my non-traditional home life, I was doing well on the surface. We moved a couple of times after his divorce until we finally settled into a home that felt like it could be a second chance. He promised he would make some changes and be a better dad. I became pretty familiar with the serenity prayer and a specific twelve steps when he occasionally practiced them.

With great expectations, our new house represented a "clean" start, in more ways than one. For a brief time, he seemed to be trying. He would leave some money on the counter and tell me it was for dinner. I got used to eating out—alone. I frequented a deli that I would walk to and get my favorite sandwich. I created my own routine, which included meeting up with friends here and there. The most popular meeting spot, the "Butte," was where you could always find someone to hang out with.

If you had a license to drive, you "cruised the Butte" (pronounced *byoot*). Box Butte Avenue was the main strip in town. Lined with bricks, the road made a magical and subtle sound with gentle vibrations as cars and trucks slowly passed over it. With windows rolled down and music turned up, everyone tried to look their best while the parade of vehicles showcased who was dating who, what fight was about to go down, where the party was happening, and if the cops were out "fishing."

It was where hands repeatedly flipped up from steering wheels as friends greeted each other on the same loop. We spent every Friday and Saturday night cruising up and down the strip waving at the same people over and over again. Occasionally, you would pull over and chat with friends, make plans, or find out what was going on later that night, but cruising the Butte was the thing to do.

Remember, my friends thought my dad was so cool and he embraced and enjoyed the attention. He had a dark cherry Iroc-Z with T-tops and would ask me if I wanted to cruise the Butte in it with him. I remember going for a drive with him once and finding ourselves smack dab in the mix of a high school cruise, and the attention he sought disgusted me. Cars full of girls would wave at him and sweetly call out "hi" in their young, cheerful voices. Seeing his eyes light up and his dimples exposed as he smiled left me ill. I never again went for a ride with him on the weekend, fearing where we would end up, knowing he used me as an admission ticket.

We lived on a residential street, just blocks from downtown and within walking distance to several of my friends. Although not perfect, things seemed to be improving. It was not long after we moved in that Diana rang the doorbell and asked if she could use the phone because hers wasn't working. "Of course," I said as I opened the door wider and waved my hand to welcome her in. Diana lived directly across the street from us, and although I recognized her from school, I didn't know her until that day.

Diana was a tough girl, the kind you didn't mess with. She smoked Marlboro Reds, wore a leather jacket, and had drug store bleached blonde hair. I was sixteen at the time (she turned seventeen before I did)—but Diana looked older. I introduced her to my father, and from that moment, she seemed to have a liking for me. Confused and a bit nervous by the subsequent chain of events, I recall being completely shocked when she asked if I wanted to have a sleepover.

Uninterested but not wanting to offend her, I said, "Uh, sure. That would be cool." Unaware of where or when she was thinking, I was even more surprised when she said she would go home to get some things and come back over! What was I going to do? I was panicking. I had nothing in common with her and had no idea what to even talk about. I struggled to make conversation just in those few moments; how would I fill an entire evening?

She came back with a bag, and we watched a little TV and had some snacks. The feeling of being trapped with someone I didn't want to hang out with in my own home was crippling. When we finally went to bed, I was relieved because I had run out of things to say and was tired of trying to find ways to fill the time.

I woke up in the middle of the night to go to the bathroom and discovered she wasn't in my room. I walked to the bathroom, thinking she also woke to use the restroom, and found she wasn't in there either. As I sat on the toilet in the dark, I thought, *maybe she went home*. Either way, I wasn't upset. . . until I overheard noises coming from my father's bedroom.

Forbidden love appeared to have been premeditated and well-orchestrated. I felt like a fool, and the snacks we consumed earlier felt like they were on their way up. I wanted to run away and never come back. In the morning, I pretended like I didn't know anything because she and my dad pretended nothing had happened. I felt disgusted and wasn't sure what to do.

My junior year in high school was torturous. It was the biggest secret in town, although I knew some were aware. Diana's parents were divorced, and she lived with her mom and stepdad across from us. She didn't have many boundaries. The belief that "age is just a number" seemed to be one that her family supported, most noticeably when Diana, along with my father, suggested that I meet her single father!

In my mind, it's one thing to fail miserably as a parent, but to then offer your daughter up to a middle-aged man in an attempt to even the score or feel better about yourself and your choices was an all-new low that I never expected. There was no more hiding their "love" from me and hoping I would keep my mouth shut.

I escaped home life and the dysfunction of it all at school. That ended when Diana began passing me notes in class covered with her lip imprints on them and asking me to give them to my dad. It's not surprising that my stomach issues began in high school.

My father was a self-absorbed, selfish, alcoholic sex addict with a temper. We had an unspoken understanding that I wouldn't say anything about their relationship, and he would let me go to my best friend's house to escape whenever I wanted. My options were limited. I could go back to New York and live with my mom, or I could try my best to ignore everything and just use him as a place to live while I finished high school.

One summer night, I had plans to meet up with my friends at the county fair in the next town, about twenty miles from our house. I'd had a ride, but something happened, and my friend couldn't go at the last minute. I asked my father if I could take his Bronco, but he also wanted to go. He made a deal with me; "You can drive, but we're going too." I was desperate and took him up on the offer.

I jumped in the driver's seat, and without hesitation, they both got in the back. I put the key in the ignition, looked ahead, and just drove. I turned on some music and tried to distract myself. Neither of them said a word to me as they sat close together holding hands. I couldn't wait to get to the fair and move far away from them. I tried to think about the fun I would have with my friends and all we planned. It was a beautiful night—the kind of night that's perfect for rolling down the windows, turning up the music, and watching the dirt fly up from the road behind you.

The temperature was perfect, and it reminded me of summer nights up at Memie and Boppie's. As I drove, I could hear lips smacking and, from the corner of my eye, could see hands moving. Even with the music turned up and the windows rolled down, groaning began to surface. My stomach turned inside out, and my heart sank to a depth I never knew before. I had envisioned driving directly into a ditch, but that quickly dissipated as I considered my plans and the future I wanted to pursue.

As appealing as the idea was to hurt them like they were hurting me, I would never do that. Instead, I allowed my mind to release the pain I held inside. As they continued fondling each other, I tried even harder to fix my eyes on the road. It was like seeing a horrible accident—you never forget the gory details.

About halfway there, he told me to turn down one of the dirt roads that stem from the main road. I assumed he had to go to the bathroom or something. As we got further down the dirt road, he told me to pull over and said that they needed a minute alone to chat. He asked me if I could give them a few minutes of privacy.

What? I thought to myself. *Where did he expect me to go or do out in the middle of nowhere?* Not to mention, I was in a hurry. I had friends waiting for me, and I just wanted to get there and get out of that truck already, but I had no choice. I was in the middle of the country with nowhere to go and no way to reach anyone. He held the power and the keys.

Frustrated and furious, I tried my best to maintain composure and jumped out without saying a word. I began walking down the dirt road in front of the truck. I paced back and forth as I kicked small rocks from one place to the other. I looked up at the sky with a head full of questions and a heart full of pain and confusion. *What am I going to do?* I asked myself. "God…what am I going to do?" I posed the question out of desperation and fear, hoping, then nearly demanding, an answer.

As I continued to look up, I couldn't help but marvel at the big, beautiful, vast sky and all the bright stars that began to fill the growing darkness. At that moment, completely mesmerized and lost in the magnitude and beauty of the galaxy, I was somewhere else. No longer stuck on the side of a country road with the steamy windows of a Bronco behind me, God immersed me in a bigger world that presented greater possibilities.

It was as if looking up and seeing the vastness of the universe delivered me from the place of pain I was in and showed me another, better version of my life. While dust from the dirt road was still in motion around me, my mind fixated on a time and place beyond it. I could see and feel the possibilities that existed ahead for me as I looked up into the night. The sky held hope, wonder, and light.

As I talked to God and looked up at all He created, I knew that where I was standing and what I was enduring was temporary, and something beautiful would come of it. That night, "It will be ok," was what I heard and held onto.

As I turned around and began to head back towards the truck, I got a glimpse of something that told me it wasn't time yet. I decided that it was always better to LOOK UP and trust in a bigger plan. Firm and steady, wandering yet unwavering, I found my way. I learned that a rock could either weigh me down or be the firm ground on which I stood. How I chose to view and use the stones in my life would dictate whether I sank or sailed.

Play Track 10 (Like A Rock – Bob Seger) in Broken Little Believer Playlist

Baggage Check:

Are you carrying painful luggage with you from the past? Can you let it go and see the purpose in painful experiences?

_____

_____

_____

_____

_____

_____

_____

_____

_____

_____

_____

_____

CHAPTER 11

I Won't Back Down

I was fortunate to have had the encouragement of teachers who saw something in me where I experienced a shortage of parental support. More times than not, it was later in life that I would learn about their feelings of pride in my resilience, strength, and determination. It was common for me to run out the door for school and pass a mirror on the kitchen counter with powder lines on it and a razorblade nearby.

"It must have been some night," I thought before heading off to school. When I could take no more, feeling like I was suffocated by the twisted relationship I was forced to witness, two words slipped out of my mouth one night. "I'm telling!"

At the top of the stairs, he grabbed my neck, squeezed, and threatened to kill me if I ever said anything about their relationship. Breaking free, I ran out the front door crying, trying to catch my breath as I wandered down the dark street, wondering what I was going to do. A van happened to drive by and slowed down as it pulled up near me. I wiped my face as I nervously wondered why it was slowing down and driving alongside me. It was a bunch of kids I knew, and as they opened the sliding door, loud music and lots of fun rolled from the custom van.

A few years older than me (they were seniors when I was a freshman), I knew them all; we were friends, and I hung out with a lot of them. Of the familiar faces, Ronnie had one of the kindest souls you would ever encounter behind a rough and tough exterior. He was always kind to me and looked out for me. Ronnie got out of the van and asked me what was wrong. I just stood there crying on the sidewalk as he hugged me and told me that everything would be ok.

Unaware that I was upset because Ronnie was shielding me a bit, and it was dark, the chants of "Shane, come on!" "Get in!" and "Let's go!" filled the silent street and eventually persuaded me to get in. I learned they were heading to a party. I had no interest in partying that night, and my mind was preoccupied with what had happened and what I was going to do. As everyone hung outside by a bonfire and enjoyed the keg, Ronnie stayed by my side and consoled me rather than join in the Friday night fun.

I had nothing to rush home to and no curfew, so we all bunked there (I didn't have much choice without a car or a sober driver). My father's rules were simple—do whatever you want, and I'll do what I want. I think he thought that if he were loose with his boundaries, I would never question or disapprove of his actions, but the lack of limits encouraged me to create and enforce my own.

I felt vulnerable and uncared for, and it would later hit me in the face like a ton of bricks when my father offered my boyfriend in for a beer. He was a senior high school jock and thought my father was so cool, but what was supposed to be one of the most sacred moments of a girl's life, although often a mistake made too soon, became one of humiliation and disgust when my father asked him if he had "popped my cherry." There was nothing about my father that I liked or respected, and his example as a father was piss poor.

My father's forbidden fling ended, and he quickly found another woman to marry. She was another blond who, along with her two kids, prepared to move in with us. Thrilled he had found a more appropriate relationship and hoping it would be a more positive one since she was a mother, it seemed to me like a good start.

However, it soon became abundantly clear that she didn't have half the heart, brains, or interest in me as Mandy did. Instead of getting to know me, she saw me as an impediment to her perfect little family. His track record showed that I was disposable, and his priorities quickly shifted to embrace the priorities of whatever woman he was with. Blondy made it known that she wanted me gone, and my father was eager to accommodate her wish.

Shortly after Blondy moved in, my dear friend Ronnie, who had moved to Denver after graduating, tragically passed away in an automobile accident. He was just getting his life together, had enrolled in college, and his future was bright and promising. I was devastated by the news, and as I stayed in Ronnie's room while in Denver for his service, I found a picture of me that he kept, along with a note I had written to him thanking him for being so special to me and such a good friend.

I had lost someone extraordinary—someone who understood and cared for me and that I understood and cared for. Ronnie was too young to die, and I hated that some people had misunderstood him. I wished I could have told him how much he meant to me at least one more time. When I returned home, I wrote about Ronnie and heaven and loss as I always had. Rather than consoling me or asking me how I was doing, my father said he wanted to take me somewhere. It was a surprise.

I thought my dad was finally beginning to realize that he had a daughter standing before him that he had been ignoring for years and that perhaps he was trying to build a relationship. We got to a massive, dark building, and I began to feel nervous when he pressed a buzzer and reported that Shane was here.

Like a dog brought to a shelter, I began to squirm and fidget; my breath became shallow, and I swallowed over and over again. I asked my dad, "What is this place?" but he didn't answer me. When we reached the end of the hallway, a woman greeted us and escorted us into a room.

"Welcome, Shane. We are going to take good care of you." the woman said. I looked at my father, and he smirked. I said, "What? What do you mean take care of me?" She proceeded to tell me that my father had reported depressed and suicidal behavior and that I was being admitted into a mental hospital!

I immediately began to run, but someone in the facility grabbed me and brought me back to the room. I was a straight-A student with lots of friends. "I'm not the one who sleeps with underage women and does drugs!" I said as he smiled and told her that I was delusional and combative.

I was angry and scared. I begged and pleaded, but nothing changed, that was until I said, "I want to call my mom!" With a look of disbelief and confusion on her face, the woman who was about to admit me turned to my father and said, "I thought she didn't have a mom." Frantically, I told her, "I do have a mom. She lives in New York, and she's going to be really upset when she finds out about this!"

The woman agreed to allow me a phone call. When my mom answered the phone, I was hysterical, and she struggled to understand me. "Mom! Mom! He's trying to commit me!" I frantically sobbed. My mom, terrified, insisted nervously, "What's wrong? Slow down! Are you ok? What happened?"

Speaking faster than she could keep up with or comprehend, I rushed to tell her that Scott was trying to have me committed into a mental institution.

"WHAT?" she screamed. "That bastard!" "Let me speak to someone there!" My mother demanded to speak to the woman at the facility and told her that Scott didn't have any right to commit me as she was my legal guardian and they could do nothing without her consent.

Thank God for my mom. Thank God she was home and answered the phone. I was saved, and just in the nick of time. My relief quickly turned to fear again when I was "free to go" and realized I had to get back into the car with my father. That was the longest, scariest ride of my life. He was angry.... furious that his plan to get rid of me was foiled. By the time I got home, Blondy had successfully thrown my clothes and all of my belongings into the front yard with an order to GET OUT!

And so, I left—no car, no money, and nowhere to go. I took up temporary residence on the couch of one friend's house and then another's basement. Eventually, the school got word of my displacement. I was underage. I was a junior in high school, bound and determined to finish high school where I started. My mother wanted me to come back to New York, but I knew that wasn't the best choice either.

Scott was not going to run me out of town, and he would not control my future. I was braver and more intelligent than he knew, and I was going to succeed.

After gathering my belongings from the front yard, I spent a few weeks hopping between friend's houses. Small towns are filled with gossip. The school must have gotten wind of my situation and learned that I had not only been raising myself but was now technically homeless.

Knowing that I needed a more appropriate living arrangement than a friend's couch, the guidance counselor asked me if I could, or wanted, to go back to New York. I shared how

I had traveled and moved my entire life and just wanted to finish high school where I started. As a minor, it was now the school's responsibility to notify the state.

Numerous meetings later, a hearing took place between my father and the state to determine my care. My father claimed that he had no money to help support me and that if I lived on my own, he was unable to contribute any funding. With me was my guidance counselor, along with one of my teachers, who took considerable interest in ensuring that I would be okay.

I was advised of my options: One, I could return to New York. I was fully aware of the anger and consequences I would likely face if I returned from Nebraska. Two, I could request emancipation from my father, or three, I could become a ward of the court, also known as a foster child. This last option was absurd to me, and my least preferred. At my age and with another viable parent (although in a different state), I had no desire to live with someone I didn't even know and take on the "foster kid" label.

In light of my maturity, long-established independence, good grades, and achievements, it was deemed a possibility that I could live on my own but have the legal benefit of being a ward of the court. I didn't follow the reasoning, but my counselor explained that by opting to be a ward of the court, I would have some protection should I need it. On the other hand, should I choose to become emancipated and something happened, or I got sick, I would have no health coverage, no one to fall back on, and no way to pay medical expenses.

Conversely, if I agreed to become a ward of the court, I could live independently due to my demonstrated level of responsibility but have a safeguard should anything catastrophic or unpredicted occur. I would have all of the rights and obligations of an adult, but on paper, the state would be my technical guardian.

```
            IN THE COUNTY COURT OF            COUNTY, NEBRASKA
                        JUVENILE DIVISION

    In The Interest Of            )                 Page 103
                                  )
    Shane              , A        )        JOURNAL ENTRY
    Juvenile Under 18 Years of    )
    Age.                          )

         October 7, 1991, this matter came on for hearing on support.
    Present in court were Shane                   , her father,
                     , and                       , County Attorney of
    Box Butte County, Nebraska.
         The Court finds that                      has insufficient
    income to pay a monthly support payment, so no support is
    required.                        shall continue to make payments
    for dental work and shall continue providing health insurance for
    Shane                .                     informed the Court
    he will attempt to provide a vehicle for Shane               .
         No visitation is required, but the Court suggests that after
    a vehicle is provided to Shane that         and Shane either (1)
    obtain family mediation; (2) obtain family counseling; or (3)
    schedule regular meetings together, hopefully once a week.
         IT IS ORDERED.

                              BY THE COURT:

    FILED

    COUNTY COURT

    OCT 2 4 1991
```

So, as a senior in high school, I lived in my own apartment, worked two jobs to pay rent, maintained high grades, and received academic achievement awards. I had many friends and was well-liked, but it was difficult for me to act my age—especially knowing I had to work, pay bills, and figure out how I would get to school when my unreliable but affordable car broke down.

I derived satisfaction from doing things other people thought I couldn't. When they doubted me, I turned it into motivation. My sweetest satisfaction? I knew my father's morning routine was pouring a cup of coffee and drinking it while reading the daily newspaper.

This awareness motivated me to be featured in the paper as often as I could. In that rinky-dink town paper, highlights of students who had achieved a certain GPA, earned various recognitions, or accomplished something special, were highlighted in print.

In my senior year alone, I made the paper over ten times for various things, including being named Student of the Week several times, Renaissance Student of the Day, and making the quarterly honor roll. The Girls' Choir received a distinguished invitation to compete at the state level, and I was recognized for my solo in the Girls Glee club when we sang *Wind Beneath My Wings* to the veterans.

The biggest whopper of them all will be revealed later. He may have thrown me out and traded me for another woman and her two children, but I was determined to remind him of the spirit he could never destroy.

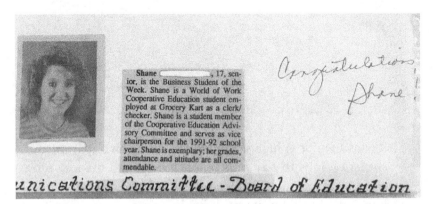

Shane _____, 17, senior, is the Business Student of the Week. Shane is a World of Work Cooperative Education student employed at Grocery Kart as a clerk/checker. Shane is a student member of the Cooperative Education Advisory Committee and serves as vice chairperson for the 1991-92 school year. Shane is exemplary; her grades, attendance and attitude are all commendable.

Congratulations, Shane!

...nications Committee - Board of Education

Shane

is the

Renaissance Student of the Day

for

Excellence in Education

February 12, 1992

Principal

HIGH SCHOOL

Honor Award

This Is To Certify That

SHANE

has been awarded this Certificate for

Outstanding Achievement

in Language Arts ~ Student of the Week

Given this 27th day of April 19 92

PRINCIPAL

HIGH SCHOOL

Honor Award

This Is To Certify That

SHANE

has been awarded this Certificate for

Outstanding Achievement

in Business ~ Student of the Week

Given this 16th day of December 1991

PRINCIPAL

119

WIND BENEATH MY WINGS — The ▓▓▓▓▓ High School girls glee club sings in tribute to the ▓▓▓▓▓ County servicemen who were stationed in Saudi Arabia during the Persian Gulf War.

SHANE

Age: 18 - Senior

Language Arts - Student of the Week

Shane has worked hard as a student aide in the speech and theatre department this year. Shane has gone above and beyond in her work, showing excellent skills in organization of time by finishing all tasks given well in advance of a deadline. Her work on the computer or bulletin board has shown that she is a competent, creative and imaginative student. As Shane is a senior, her talents shall be missed next year.

Play Track 11 (I Won't Back Down – Tom Petty) in Broken Little Believer Playlist

Baggage Check:

Among your luggage, is there a particular piece you carry with you that motivates you to keep going? Can you recall a time in your life when others doubted you, but you were determined to succeed?

_____

_____

_____

_____

_____

_____

_____

_____

_____

_____

_____

SECTION 3

Lost and Disoriented
(Chapters 12-16)

There are many times in life when we face roadblocks, feel lost, or have to reconfigure our travel plans. We can view these unexpected interruptions, delays, and detours as burdens or blessings. Running out of gas, losing the map, asking for directions, misplacing our keys, or taking an alternate route are crucial parts of the journey. The total experience brings us closer to finding the path we are meant to travel while learning to appreciate unexpected views and unplanned adventures along the way.

CHAPTER 12

Fire and Rain

I used to hate being alone and would often get in my car and just drive around aimlessly to escape the lonely walls that surrounded me. Amy Grant's "If These Walls Could Speak" and Pink Floyd's "Wish You Were Here" were among the songs I played over and over again in my apartment. They became a part of my life's soundtrack, keeping me motivated and preventing me from going to a dark place in my mind. I couldn't risk going there. I knew that if I did, I would have to rely on myself to find a way out, and life was already hard enough. I didn't need any more challenges.

I made a trip back to New York once while I lived in my apartment in Nebraska, and my budget indicated that the best choice would be to get there by Greyhound bus. I had become quite the traveler. What would have scared others was exciting to me. I spent days traveling on a bus to get from Nebraska to New York. The trip was broken up only by quick stops for leg stretching and running into gas station convenience stores. Besides the many different smells, such as exhaust, commercial commode deodorizer, and of course, the all-natural and often ripe mixture of body odors, I enjoyed traveling by bus. I discovered many parts of our country that I would not have otherwise seen.

I found traveling by bus to be one big adventure. I embraced the freedom, choice of destination, and knowing that nothing is ever permanent. Not knowing who I would meet, where fellow travelers were coming from or headed, what the purpose or circumstances of their trips were—it was all a mystery. I had traveled by bus before, and with each trip, every stop, and many bus changes came new experiences, introductions, and goodbyes.

Whenever I traveled by bus, it felt like a year's worth of living had taken place between the time I first boarded the bus and the moment I stepped off. More than just the extended amount of time it took to make the trip, it was all the things I had experienced within those miles that made it feel like I'd learned a lifetime of lessons.

People of all walks of life got on and off the bus, and while everyone was traveling for a different purpose, we all shared the same path for a short time. Traveling by Greyhound Bus is not for everyone, but I appreciated the opportunities it gave me to see many places and meet so many people. If cell phones and social media had been around back then, I have no doubt that I would still be in contact with many of those with whom I shared meaningful conversations.

Some of the best conversations happened in the middle of the night when I couldn't sleep, or the sounds and forward motion of the bus braking woke me. There was always someone else who was awake and wanting to chat. In the mornings, I observed passengers' many different routines by looking up and down the bus aisle. I appreciated this closeness and the sense of camaraderie that naturally formed. A communal mindset seemed to exist among passengers as everyone recognized that our different journeys brought us together to travel the same road.

I will never forget the night I met Dylan. Making our approach into the Chicago terminal, the bus driver announced, "Last Stop." As he listed the various connections offered at the station, I collected my things and made my way down the stairs. After freshening up in the station's restroom, I walked through the busy terminal, located my next bus, and proceeded to board.

It was the middle of the night, yet a bustling time for travelers and those changing buses. At the top of the landing, I scanned the bus and searched for an open seat. As I made my way down the center row, Dylan looked up, and without saying a word, moved his backpack from the aisle seat so I could sit down. He looked a lot like how I felt.

He was casual and relaxed, wearing a Mexican Baja poncho, and despite his tired appearance, seemed to have a quiet curiosity about him. We rode together for a day and a half, yet it seemed much longer. I felt like I already knew him. He was soft-spoken and deliberate with his words. Unafraid of silence, there was no awkwardness or sense of urgency to fill quiet moments. Instead, deep thoughts and profound conversations filled the hours. When my tired head unintentionally fell on his shoulder, he just smiled as he padded it with an extra sweatshirt to make it softer.

In between dozing, I woke and saw him staring out the window with his headphones on. Seeing that I was awake, he took his headphones off and handed them to me. After placing them on my ears and returning a nod to signal I was ready, he pressed "play" on his Walkman. As the chords of a sweet guitar filled my senses, I was immediately entranced by James Taylor's *Fire and Rain*.

As I listened to the song, we both shook our heads, acknowledging the validity and truth of the words. The music resonated in ways I couldn't describe, but as we shared the rest of the trip, we formed an unspoken connection neither of us needed to try and explain. As the bus continued down the road, the words of the song played in my head. I have listened to that song many times and found the lyrics to be uncannily on point.

"I've seen lonely times when I could not find a friend, but I always thought that I'd see you again."[4] Just as I found comfort in the simple gift of leaning on his shoulder while I slept and he on mine, I found comfort in knowing that there are many people in this world with whom we share instant connections. If we are genuine in our interactions, these connections, no matter how long or brief, become gifts that stay with us forever.

Play Track 12 (Fire and Rain – James Taylor) in Broken Little Believer Playlist

Baggage Check:

Do you carry a memory of someone that brings you comfort? Is that memory so cherished or so poignant that it has the power to transport you back to that moment in time?

_____

_____

_____

_____

_____

_____

_____

_____

_____

_____

_____

_____

CHAPTER 13

Homecoming Queen

While living on my own in high school, I learned many hard lessons earlier than most. I was already very responsible, but because my name was the only thing guaranteeing rental agreements and payment plans, I prepared to be even more so. I often shopped at the Reservation Mission Store, a thrift shop that benefited local Native Americans.

Once a week, they had "Bag Sales," and I could fill a brown paper bag with anything in the store for five dollars. My area of focus? Men's dress jackets. I would fill my bag with as many blazers and suit jackets as I could – tweed, corduroy, wool, you name it. I had found a way to make jeans and blazers look good, and it serendipitously became my thing.

No one knew the source of my wardrobe or how thrifty and creative I could be, but I made it work while supporting a cause that was close to home and my heart. I got to know the woman who worked there during my weekly shopping trips, and she always expected me—especially on bag sale days. Even when my bags' contents would sometimes spill over the top, she justified the amount in them since I was buying large men's jackets. She was a thoughtful and generous woman.

Not long after I moved into my apartment, I received some mail that left me feeling embarrassed and ashamed. With a return address that read, "State of Nebraska," inside, I found a small packet of colorful coupons tucked inside the envelope. It reminded me of Monopoly money that had been stapled together. As I looked closer at the packet, I saw the words "food stamps" printed on it and quickly turned the outside of the envelope over to reinspect the address.

Convinced it was a mistake or that I had inadvertently opened someone else's mail, upon seeing my name, I called the only contact I had from the hearing and asked why I received this. I qualified for a small ration of food stamps due to my income. Refusing to use them, I ripped the stubs up and threw them away. Going grocery shopping for myself was already an uncomfortable task. Using government assistance and handing over food coupons would only call even greater attention to myself and my situation.

A good friend happened to be over one day after I had checked my mail. Upset by the sight of another envelope containing a new month's worth of food stamps, my girlfriend observed a change in my demeanor and asked me what was wrong. I confided in her that I was upset that the state sent these to me, and I didn't want them. I told her I was ripping them up and throwing them away.

"WHY?" she asked, "You should use them!" Embarrassed, I told her that there was "NO WAY" that I would be caught using food stamps. I certainly didn't look down on anyone who had to use them. For most of our life, my mom qualified for them, but she was too proud to accept the assistance. In my mind, my strength would be compromised if I took this help. I was testing myself and wanted to prove that I could do it, I could survive. Just the sight of the vouchers reminded me of a dark time and a future that felt limited. I didn't want to be comfortable. It was in my struggle that I discovered my strength.

On the other hand, my friend thought it was the greatest thing and suggested that if I weren't going to use them, she would! I ended up giving them to her, and she had a blast shopping for free food. These vouchers didn't represent anything other than some extra snacks for her and other hungry teenagers, but for me, they reminded me of my reality. We made a new routine, and I began giving them to her since she had no aversion to using them. Eventually, I came to accept some canned vegetables, milk, and bread that she picked up for me while she shopped for fun snacks during her personal shopping service.

I didn't fear being alone, but I did get lonely. While my friends all went home to their families, I would go home to my apartment and stare at the walls. Deciding what to eat for dinner was always tough. I ate a lot of canned vegetables. My favorite was either canned green beans or peas. I would drain the liquid, pour them in a bowl, microwave them, and put a big slab of butter on the hot veggies. I lived on that (and peanut butter and jelly sandwiches). The best was when a friend would invite me over for dinner. I don't think they ever knew how much those meals meant or how good they tasted to me.

My living room window overlooked a large, open field. Living in tornado country, I wasn't surprised to be awoken by alarms notifying residents of a tornado warning or spotting one in the area. When you live in Nebraska, you become acutely aware of the weather, and even subtle changes in the sky are cause for notice and possible concern. I had seen funnel clouds just outside my window, and I was fascinated and concerned all at the same time.

To watch dirt gently float with the wind and then magically and swiftly begin to oscillate, transforming into a small whipping cylinder of circular motion, is impressive but scary.

I could see these little funnels start to take shape from my window, and I never knew if they would dissipate or grow larger and become more powerful. When the alarms went off, residents would all take their place in the hallways and hunker down until the storm warning passed.

At times like these, I wished I had someone to offer a comforting word or a reassuring embrace, but I often focused my attention on the elderly neighbors who also lived alone and felt the same fear. I remembered that I was alone but recognized that I wasn't the only one.

In the silence of that tiny apartment, I did a lot of soul searching. I often wondered how my life would turn out. How would I go to college? Would I meet the right guy and, one day, have a family? How many kids would I have? What would I do with my life, and what kind of career did I want? What was my purpose? That last question always seemed to burn a bit and demand a more immediate answer. I revisited that question often.

It seemed whenever I considered my purpose, I replayed everything that had happened in my life and how I'd overcome obstacles. I wondered how my personal trials and challenges would allow me to help someone else one day. I had always convinced myself that there was a reason for everything, and maybe, just maybe, I was going through certain things so that I could better understand or help someone else.

As graduation drew closer, how and where I was going to college became a growing concern. While many were going on campus tours, finalizing school decisions, and making preparations, I was just trying to pay my rent each month. For me, there was no discussion about college, where I wanted to go, or even what I wanted to study, and things like tuition, financial aid, and registration deadlines were foreign to me. I knew nothing. No one in my family had gone to college, so there was no pre-existing knowledge or experience from which to draw.

Just a few months shy of high school graduation, I received a call on my apartment phone. A woman introduced herself as a pageant director. Susan said she had received several letters from people in my community nominating me to compete in a pageant. Almost laughing at what felt like a joke, I listened as Susan described how the letters had a consistent theme. They contained comments about my drive and role as a positive leader among young people.

I scoffed at the word "pageant" and the idea of a beauty contest. "Still," Susan went on, "to be in this particular competition, a person needs nominations for their positive contributions within their community." Uncomfortable with the topic, I let out a nervous laugh and just said, "No, thank you. I've never been in a pageant, and they really aren't my thing."

She insisted that outer appearance was only part of it and that academic achievement and leadership among young women were the focus of this pageant. Still not warm to the idea, I thanked her for her call and said that I didn't think it was for me. She gave me her number to call back, should I reconsider, and invited me to use it. I never did.

Weeks went by, and to my surprise, Susan called me again. She made the point that college scholarships were among the possible awards and prizes the contest offered. Still struggling with the idea of a pageant, I told her I needed to think about it.

Time was ticking, and my college opportunities were limited to none, so I will admit, she had me intrigued. Even if I had considered it, though, I had no car, as mine was broken beyond repair, and the pageant took place at a location over six hours away. Not to mention the most obvious—I did not have the experience, resources, or support to compete with those who were much more prepared for such an event.

I decided to consult with my favorite English teacher, Mrs. B, and she encouraged me to give it a shot. She even loaned me her car to get there! I needed three outfits: an evening gown, which someone in town made for me and donated as a token of good luck, an interview outfit, and a fun, sporty ensemble.

With little money, I set off to do some shopping and found a few pieces that would work. The interview outfit, a "Blue Light Special" from Kmart, and the sporty outfit (a combination of things I already owned and borrowed from a friend) made up my pageant wardrobe. Ready or not, I set off to discover what the event would bring with nothing more than a tank full of gas. With great care, I placed the three outfits that I had pressed and hung importantly on wire hangers and laid them delicately in the back.

In doing so, I discovered that my teacher's family had put a surprise fruit basket together for me and placed it on the backseat. It was a gesture that made me smile from ear to ear. After a long, tension-filled drive, I arrived at the venue and nervously walked into the packed auditorium.

Instantly feeling like a fish out of water, I hesitantly made my way down the center aisle of the large room and couldn't help but notice all the beautiful girls. Pods of people were spread out all over the auditorium, and within them were girls and their family members. Some even had hairdressers and seamstresses, and of course, friends and homemade signs to cheer them on.

Here I was, all alone, with nothing but my outfits draped over my shoulder, my bent fingers gripping their hangers. I was out of my element, and my nerves were at an all-time high. I decided I couldn't do it. I turned around and began to walk out.

At that moment, a woman who worked with the pageant association approached me and asked me my name as she held a clipboard and offered to check me in. I told her I wasn't staying and followed it with, "I shouldn't be here."

Sensing my nervousness, the woman gently placed her hand on my arm, tapping a time or two, and reassured me I would be "just fine." When she asked me where my family was, I could tell she did her best to disguise the surprise when I replied that they weren't there. She quickly introduced me to some other girls, hoping that I would begin to feel a little more comfortable.

As I went through the interview process, which was the part of the pageant with which I felt most comfortable, surprise seemed to fall over the judges as I deftly answered the questions they created for the competition. Unaware at the time, it surprised me when the judges later commented on how mature and well-spoken I was and that I didn't sound like an eighteen-year-old girl.

I continued in the event, closely watching the other girls and taking note of how they walked, turned, and waved, and I successfully completed all areas of the competition. The moment arrived when we were all called to take the stage and line up. As we stood side by side, holding hands, the announcer began to congratulate us all for making it that far. I just knew that I was going home empty-handed, but I was relieved that it was over. Oddly, I felt a new sense of pride for doing something I didn't think I could do.

One by one, the officials announced the winners by level. They started with the junior level, the younger girls, and then moved onto the senior level, the sixteen to eighteen-year-olds. With each name they called, I became more and more convinced that I would be going home soon. If I wasn't the fourth, third, or second runner-up, I knew it was over.

I was the big loser. I stood there with thoughts flooding through my mind. *What were you thinking? Did you actually believe you could win something? What an idiot!* I couldn't wait for this to be over so that I could get in the car and drive home. As they built suspense around the announcement of the future Miss Teen Nebraska, I felt like it was cruel and unusual punishment to be forced to stand there any longer.

I was about to cry, wondering anew how I would get to college. As I stood there, internally beating myself up, the announcer said, "And the winner of the Miss Nebraska National Teenager title, hailing from our state's panhandle, is Shane" I didn't even hear him say my last name. The auditorium had erupted into applause as soon as the first name left the announcer's lips. I did not respond immediately because the applause and the voices in my head were so loud and distracting, I honestly didn't believe or expect it. The girl standing next to me nudged me and said, "Shane, you won!"

Shocked and nearly frozen in place thinking it was a dream, realizing what I'd just heard, I began jumping up and down on stage, so NOT what a pageant queen does. Fortunately, they didn't seem to mind but did tell me not to do that at the Miss Teen USA pageant.

I tried to collect myself and did my best wave after being crowned and presented with a trophy and a big bouquet of flowers. As people took pictures of me with my sash, trophy, and crown, someone asked me if a family member would like to accompany me on stage. Not having anyone in attendance with me, I hurried off the stage, called my mom, and told her the news.

"I won! I won!" I screamed through the phone as she excitedly screamed just as loud in return. The entire experience was surreal. I drove all the way home, never once taking my crown or sash off. Smiling all the way to my teacher's driveway, I jumped up and down in excitement as she answered the front door and saw that I had been crowned the winner.

Newly crowned.

I received a two-year scholarship to Oklahoma, where I was going to study to be a nurse. It was a natural career choice. I loved people and wanted to make them feel better. Graduation was approaching, and I continued to work two jobs and finish up school. I needed to earn and save all the money I could.

While friends were going out and having their last hoorahs as seniors, I remembered feeling a little left out. It bothered me a bit, but I focused on the bigger picture and was grateful to be going to college. There were nights I worked at Taco John's, and a carload of friends would come through the drive-thru to place their order.

Once they knew it was me, they would all start yelling in the speaker, "Hey Shane! Come out with us when you finish your shift!" I could hear all the fun they were having as I took their order, and thought how nice it would be to meet up with them later. But I would have to go home and take a shower since the smell of potato oles and bean burritos is not attractive. By the time I closed the store, it would be too late, and I had to work the next day. Not many people realized the life I led in high school, or so I thought.

It was the night before graduation, and I had just pressed my gown. I was excited and nervous at the same time. I couldn't believe I was about to graduate high school and would soon be leaving for college. Sitting alone in my apartment imagining my future felt surreal. A faint knock at the door jolted me from my deep thoughts.

When I opened it, I found my friend, who had graduated a couple of years before me and lived in the apartment upstairs, standing before me with blood dripping from his arms. He had tried to slit his wrists and was standing there, speechless and with a look of confusion on his face.

Panicked, I called 911 as I talked to him and asked him what happened and why he did this. He didn't give me a definitive answer, but I had some ideas. Fighting back the tears as I tried to hide my fear and worry from my friend, I made every call I could to alert emergency personnel to my apartment building.

The paramedics took him to the hospital, where he recovered from his self-sustained injuries, but that night would haunt me for a long time. At my door stood someone I knew well and deeply cared for, who felt hopeless and alone. I never forgot that night or the feelings I had of desperately wanting to help my friend in his time of need. It stayed with me as a poignant reminder that you never know what people face or the struggles they endure. I have replayed the events of that night in my head many times and have often considered what might have happened if I didn't hear that knock on the door or if I chose to ignore it. Doors have always been symbolic to me, and their existence presents a choice. Do we keep them open, do we slam them shut, do we hide behind them, or nervously stand in front of them? Sometimes, it's the littlest choices that have the most significance in our lives. I intend to keep my door open and always answer the knocks.

With graduation happening the next day, there was no opportunity to discuss the events of that night with my friend. Soon, my apartment was all boxed up, and it was time to go. Not having a car, I came up with the idea to rent a U-Haul and drive it to Oklahoma, where I would begin my college career. On the outside of the U-Haul, friends had taped several posters congratulating me on winning the title and wishing me luck at college.

As I drove myself to school, unaware of what I would find, the occasional friendly beeps and waves from other drivers who saw the signs kept me company on the road and reminded me that I wasn't alone. As I arrived in Oklahoma and pulled up to the campus that I saw for the first time, it hit me. This transition was more difficult than I had imagined. With a U-Haul filled with cheap, make-shift furniture, pots, pans, and kitchen utensils from my apartment, I soon discovered, not only was there not enough room for all of these things in my dorm, but I didn't need them.

A rollout bed with drawers underneath and a built-in wooden bookcase for my belongings made up half of the room. There was no kitchen, so there was no need for any of my dishes or other small appliances, and there certainly was no space for a sofa or the milk crates that served as small tables in my apartment. I couldn't help but feel out of place. Alone and unsure of everything, I did my best to put on a brave face.

With the help of seniors who traditionally assisted freshman move-in on Welcoming Day, we unloaded the U-Haul, brought my clothes and bedding up to my room, and scheduled another truck to come and pick up my housewares which I donated to Goodwill. I was not prepared for any of this.

I met my roommate, lovely but quiet, and always with headphones on as she listened to music. I was lost and homesick and didn't feel like I belonged. These emotions came as a surprise to me because I had spent so much time alone and now couldn't understand why this felt unusual.

I called my high school English teacher from the payphone in the hall of my dorm and told her I wanted to come back. My voice trembled as I confessed that I felt like I made a mistake. Always so kind and supportive, she reassured me that it would get better. Mrs. B knew I would make new friends and feel comfortable in no time. She told me to "give it a couple of days before making any hasty decisions" and see how I felt then.

She was right. I tried to get to know my roommate better, but she wasn't a talkative person and preferred to keep to herself. Soon, I got to know other girls in the dorm and made friends with them and other students in my classes.

During my freshman year of college, I flew to Nashville for the Miss Teen USA pageant and represented my state of Nebraska. Although I did not win, it was another experience that I won't ever forget. My platform was to help shed light and spread awareness on fostering children. Coincidentally, while at college, I received the following letter, and it completely blindsided me.

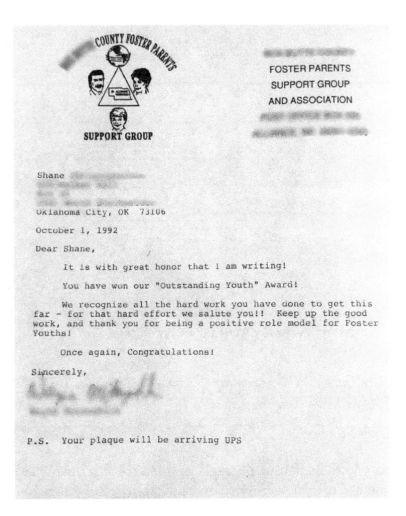

The state of Nebraska later invited me to speak to children who needed moral support and peer guidance. In addition to receiving the "Outstanding Youth" award, the Governor of Nebraska thanked me for my mentorship of other children and my positive contributions to my community.

Initially embarrassed by the recognition of my personal experience and affiliation, it later served as additional motivation to act. It deeply solidified my belief that part of my purpose is to use my pain to help others.

CONNECTION
Nebraska Youth

Miss Nebraska Teen-Ager
thanks others for success

I have lived on my own since September of 1991 as a ward of the state.

In school, I maintained an A-B grade average, and I managed to hold two jobs, along with extracurricular activities and sports involvement. I am very proud of myself for the achievements I accomplished after being removed from my home; however, living on my own throughout my senior year was tough. Because I was dedicated to my education and had the stress of bills and work, I wasn't able to do all the things that many of my friends were able to do.

While being on my own, I was chosen Business Student of the Week, Language Arts Student of the Week and Renaissance Student of the Day at my high school, Miss Congeniality at my County Fair, and I received other honors. I have worked very hard and give credit to my mother in New York for all of her support, God for my strength, and the State of Nebraska for its assistance.

When I look at the things I have done in my life, I strongly believe that it paid off in the end.

On June 27, 1992, I was chosen Miss Nebraska National Teen-Ager! It was one of the happiest days of my life. Not only was I receiving national recognition, but fantastic scholarships, also. Then I flew to Nashville, Tennessee, for the national pageant!

As Miss Nebraska National Teen-Ager, Shane

This August, she competit in the America's National Teen-Ager Pageant at Opryland in Nashville, Tennessee.

FALL · EDITION

Interview by Nebraska Connection Youth

Play Track 13 (Homecoming Queen? – Kelsea Ballerini) in Broken Little Believer Playlist

Baggage Check:

As you look at your baggage, can you recall a time when you had to start over? Did you, perhaps, let go of things you once thought were essential but realized later that you didn't need them?

_____

_____

_____

_____

_____

CHAPTER 14

Perfect

Halfway through my freshman year, I learned of an opening for a Resident Assistant (RA) in my dormitory. Traditionally, RA positions were reserved for upperclassman; however, I decided to give it a shot and apply. The stipend would come in handy, and the single room with a private bathroom—an attractive, added bonus.

The interview went well, and I was offered the position, making me the first freshman in the dorm's history to hold an RA position. The board noted my maturity, willingness to help others, eagerness to work hard, and compliance with dorm rules, prompting them to make an exception for my freshman status.

My position required me to be on call and readily available to dorm residents who might need a listening ear, assistance, or general advice. I enjoyed my job and loved the slightly larger, private room. I was back to living alone, and while it was something I had grown comfortable with over the years, I did miss out on late-night girl talks and the camaraderie that comes with having roommates. I also didn't have the opportunity to experience the freedom of being young and making mistakes without paying higher consequences for them. I had a reputation and an obligation to uphold. On the flip side, I was able to avoid much of the cattiness, gossip, and drama that often infiltrated groups of girls.

Greek life and organized clubs were the way to become more involved, and soon, I found myself going through "Rush." It was an awkward process, and I found the "sorting" of girls to be a bit demeaning. I was fortunate to be picked by my first choice, but others weren't as lucky and didn't get their first or second choice, leaving them to accept whatever group would take them. I picked up on this unspoken, long-established and accepted, stereotyping system, and it didn't sit well with me.

My sorority had a reputation for promoting respect and positive leadership. Its members were warm and welcoming, so while I acknowledged the mixed feelings I got from Greek life, I was grateful to be sworn into this chapter. Thrust into a new, highly organized arrangement of friends, I wondered why I felt out of place at times. I found it difficult to relate to some of my "sisters" and found the cost of this premium membership as a financial investment and an emotional one. It seemed my "adoption" into this sisterhood only exaggerated how different our lives were.

The family and financial support most others had left me feeling insecure and hiding who I was and where I came from. A traditional event of purchasing and exchanging "Lil Sis" and "Big Sis" sweatshirts became a choice between paying for my meal plan or participating in this highly anticipated event. Girls excitedly picked out the fabric, chose fun designs, and created one-of-a-kind personalized sweatshirts to present to their Lils and Bigs.

I so badly wanted to be part of the group, but I couldn't ignore all the obstacles I faced as I struggled to find commonality. I took out loans and applied for financial aid to pay for my books, supplies, and meal plan. I decided to go further in debt to remain part of the sorority rather than harboring feelings of not belonging, but there came a time when I could no longer pay the membership dues.

My financial hardship was handled discreetly, and most were gracious and sympathetic. I remain friends with several of my former sorority sisters to this day, but my "sisters" are still unaware of my family history or the struggles I faced then. I didn't want to accept greater responsibilities, but I chose to so I could stay in school. Forgoing time with my "sisters" due to circumstances beyond my control left me resenting that I had to make choices such as these at my age.

A brand-new student housing facility had been built, and the advantages and appeals of the newly designed apartments were many. With a modern appearance and the added safety of being on campus, this new development offered students individual lease protection within multi-bedroom apartments. Better yet, they were hiring, so I planned to apply. I didn't know this until I arrived in Oklahoma, but I landed a two-year tuition-only scholarship at one of the most expensive private universities around. I quickly realized I needed to make more money and could not take out any more student loans. I still had to pay for room, board, and books, not to mention basic living expenses. I was only eighteen, a freshman, and I was already in significant debt. I will say, though, I have NEVER eaten that well before!

My slender canned-vegetable-and-butter-eating frame took on the "freshman fifteen" in record time. It wasn't because I overindulged or ate like other college students my freshman year, but because I wasn't accustomed to eating three meals a day, having a choice of foods, or having them prepared by someone other than me. It was smorgasbord time!

After my first year as a Resident Assistant in the dorm, I applied for a position at the new housing complex and was offered the job. Part of my compensation, along with a small salary, included a free studio apartment. My mixed duties included some similar the RA position, but now I would be on-call for several buildings on alternating nights.

In addition to this responsibility, I also worked as a leasing agent in the main office, showing prospective students and their families around the property and securing new leases. I enjoyed the job and found it easy to speak to people and put new students at ease while comforting worried, anxious parents.

In between my office shifts and being on-call, which meant I carried a beeper in case of emergency, disturbance, or other student issues, I attended school full time. I took nursing courses and did clinical work and rotations at the hospital. I had been assigned a few patients and was responsible for tracking their care and providing updated reports.

I was a disciplined and determined student, but in my second year, I found that my workload was too great. My nursing instructors, a couple of shrews, seemed to give me the most challenging cases. Even some of my classmates were convinced they were trying to break me. It was difficult for me to focus only on my patients' clinical side and not see the human and emotional side of their health and how it all connected.

My "whole patient" approach irritated my instructors. Fully understanding and acknowledging the importance of measurable tests and concrete values in our training, I couldn't help but feel discouraged when there was little to no time to chat with a distraught, lonely, or scared patient. The realities of healthcare were disturbing to me. It felt cold, rushed, and impersonal.

At the time, I was devastated that my plan of becoming a nurse looked like it wasn't going to happen, but my experience was a blessing in disguise as it served to show me a different path. I have an enormous amount of respect for nurses knowing that so many invest endless hours caring for their patients with skill and compassion, only to be stretched too thin to give everyone the time and attention they desperately want and deserve.

Suffice to say, the time I spent in Oklahoma wasn't great. No matter how hard I tried to make it work, it felt like a dark cloud was hanging over me. I was just surviving. I was trying to find my way, and though I managed to fulfill all my responsibilities while putting myself through school, disappointment and uncertainty over my future grew.

That dark cloud began to envelop me. I was lost, forgot my purpose, and began to doubt myself and my value. I knew I had to make some quick changes. My two-year scholarship was coming to an end, and the student housing company where I worked was building a new property in Texas. They asked if I would consider relocating with the company since I was familiar with their housing models and had become one of their best student leasing agents.

With my personal experience living on the property as a student and my professional experience working for the company, it seemed like a natural fit when they asked me to take the lead as their preconstruction leasing agent on another college campus. Drawings and plans could conceptually give students an idea of what was coming, but I could paint the picture and describe how the finished product would look and feel. I accepted the position in Texas, which allowed me to transfer schools and find success in sales while finishing my degree. The following year, the Oklahoma City bombings took place just two miles from the university I previously attended. I was grateful my scholarship had been for two years and not three.

Coincidentally, Brad, a guy I met and began dating in Oklahoma, was hired by the athletic department at the same college in Texas and planned to relocate. It almost seemed too much of a coincidence to me. We did not make our moves simultaneously, although I did accompany him and one of his friends when he drove his belongings there. Within a few weeks, we had both made our way to Texas and settled into our own apartments.

We continued dating for a while, but inevitably, our paths were meant to go in different directions. I met Brad's family several times and had a great deal of respect for them and their values, and I wished Brad the best in his endeavors. Several years later, as fate would have it, we happened to cross paths again at another apartment complex in the same town and realized we both lived there. In the end, we were better friends than we were a couple, and our subsequent encounters and conversations consisted only of good wishes and support of one another and our big dreams.

Play Track 14 (F**kin' Perfect – Pink) in Broken Little Believer Playlist

Baggage Check:

Have you ever felt like you don't belong? Do you carry feelings of insecurity or worthlessness in your luggage? Did a change in direction or time help heal you? Do you still have work to do to repair this?

_____

_____

_____

_____

_____

_____

_____

_____

_____

_____

_____

CHAPTER 15

Stop Draggin' My Heart Around

As the seasons changed, so did my taste in guys, or so it would appear as I, unintentionally, went from a basketball coach to a baseball player. He was good looking, I guess, and we had many similar interests. I worked and attended college full-time at the University of Texas.

I didn't know how to be a carefree college student but tried to have fun when I could. My priority was to graduate as fast as possible, so I wouldn't accumulate any more student loans or college debt than necessary. I decided that I wanted to be a teacher and would get a degree in English/Communications. Without much disposable income or the receipt of parental allowances like so many other students my age, I didn't go shopping, out to eat, or to clubs very often.

Meeting guys was more challenging, too, since I was always busy. I was a serious and committed employee who depended on my job and the income it provided. Going out, getting drunk, and calling in sick were not options—although there were a few times I wished they were.

With a job that required a professional appearance, it wasn't surprising that my wardrobe was "business attire" heavy. I didn't know how to dress casually, and when friends told me to relax, it wasn't easy for me to do. When others registered for classes and excitedly bought various school sweatshirts, t-shirts, hats, and pajama bottoms at the bookstore, I bought books.

I would have loved to have had a collection of spirit wear, but my work clothes were necessary—the rest was not. When I went out, I often mixed pieces and tried to pair a button-down work shirt with a pair of jeans or wore a skirt and tried to make it more casual by adding a belt to an untucked shirt.

It was at a party that I met a guy who I later nicknamed Pants. He told some of his friends that he thought I was pretty, and word quickly reached me. I was the best-dressed (or most over-dressed) student there, and I remember feeling insecure about it. Even though we were all the same age, my circumstances felt daunting—working at a professional position rather than a more traditional college student job. I was the face of a property where many of my peers lived and partied, and my schedule left me little time to hang out with other college kids. I was out of the loop.

Nothing could have validated my feelings more than when other students at the party said, "Hey! You're the girl who works in the office, right?" It seemed no matter how cool and relaxed I tried to be, my reputation of being a mature, responsible, hard-working girl followed me, and I began to resent it.

So, when Pants took an interest in me, I was flattered and fell harder than I probably should have. Competing with other girls who, in my mind, had less baggage and more to offer, including time, I convinced myself that it was worth holding onto him. I almost felt like a regular college girl with a jock boyfriend.

After quickly falling for each other, my mind raced to the future. Excited by what my heart felt and craving normalcy, our relationship continued on an upbeat, fast track. I was afraid to miss an opportunity and truly believed that we were on our paths for a reason. Young and naive, we talked about how in love we were and what our futures looked like: where we wanted to live, how many kids we would have, the whole nine yards.

As someone who took notice of things and always believed in purpose, and as crazy as it sounds, I thought that two things were signs of our meant-to-be union. One was when I noticed that the tip of Pants' thumb was missing. Having also sustained an injury when I was little, where the tip of my thumb had been caught in a door, severed, reattached, and was slightly misshapen, I felt like it was a sign. I mean, what were the odds? The second thing was that his name contained a part of my biological father's name. At first, I thought it was a sign to run in the opposite direction but then wondered if it meant something different. I put a lot of faith in two deformed thumbs and a familiar name. Brilliant.

Pants signed on with a farm team and would soon go to Florida for spring training. Young and in love, we couldn't bear the thought of being separated. Our conversations quickly turned to marriage. We also knew that if we were married before he began his baseball career, we would stay in the married section of team housing. This arrangement was an appealing consideration to him since he wouldn't have room-mates, and for me, I trusted that things were unfolding as they should.

In January, we were married in a Baptist Church to which we didn't belong. Our friends and the school baseball team were in attendance. My mom and Chris flew in for the event, and just as I was about to walk down the aisle, Mom turned to me, looked me straight in the eyes, and said, "Are you sure you want to do this?"

I was offended and hurt by her question, but that's because she was right. I wasn't sure. We had a basic reception at a Knights of Columbus-type hall with a buffet, and the DJ was a classmate of mine. Everything about the event and our plans for the future revolved around him, and I quickly felt like it was becoming more of a never-ending party for him and his friends to enjoy than it was about our marriage.

Still, I was a doting partner and committed to doing everything I could to support him and his dream of becoming a professional baseball player. I even took extra classes at night to finish sooner while making arrangements with my professors to allow me to take my finals early so that I could accompany my husband to spring training.

I had a reliable car that I had worked hard to buy. It was sporty, fun, and probably the only age-appropriate thing I owned, and it was all mine. When we were about to move to Florida, his parents suggested we trade my car for a truck to accommodate his equipment and belongings. Not giving it much thought, I said so long to my car, and together, we took on a used wimpy, pint-sized Nissan with a cap over the bed, making it look even more unappealing. There was no doubt that I got screwed on that deal because we ended up with an older, less attractive, albeit more practical, vehicle and took on a monthly payment.

Soon, we were off to Florida. I got a job as a waitress and immediately made friends, several of whom I remain close with to this day. I also taught school during the day and substituted at a parochial school and another private school, where I met another dear friend to whom I'm still close. Coincidentally, this friend tipped me off to something about Pants that would later surface as a giant flaw I had overlooked.

Spring training went by fast, and soon, there were summer games and league travel, but we blinked, and before we knew it, the season was over. It was time to head back to Texas and prepare for the fall semester. When we returned to Texas, we moved into an apartment off campus. I figured we were married now, and that was the grown-up (and most cost-effective) thing to do.

While I continued to work and go to school, he attended school and trained. He had a small salary from the baseball organization, along with support from his parents. That fall semester seemed to fly by as I was busy cramming as many classes and credits into my schedule as I could. Many of them were evening classes I attended following my workday. Before we knew it, talk of reporting back to Florida for spring training began again. Our marriage was going well. We enjoyed going out, getting together with friends, and laughing and having fun.

I was flexible and accommodating when it came to his schedule, understanding that he was under a contract. He had a lot more free time at home than I did, and my feelings of responsibility didn't seem to lighten much despite being married. Regardless, things were going well. The spring semester had begun, and since Pants would soon be making his way down to Florida for training, we decided that he would go down ahead of me while I finished up my courses, and then I would meet him down there when the semester was over.

Although faithful and a hopeful believer, I struggled with worrying too much and soon became an expert. Beginning at a young age, I had worried about my family. I stressed about my grades. I juggled bills and wondered if I'd have enough money to pay rent. I worried about those I cared for, my future, and the ramifications of my choices. I fussed about what others thought of me, couldn't figure out where life would take us, and wondered if God still loved me.

Stomach issues were a common side effect of all of my worrying, but still, there came a time when it all caught up to me. With foils in my hair and clips holding them in sections, I was sitting in the chair at my hairdresser's station while still attending college in Texas, and that's when it happened. Out of nowhere, I had this overwhelming feeling that I had to leave; I had to go somewhere, anywhere. I couldn't sit there any longer.

I began to get hot and fidgety and felt like I couldn't breathe. My hairdresser, who happened to be a friend of mine, was concerned and offered me some water. I didn't know what was wrong, and I didn't know what to say to my friend, who desperately wanted to help and kept asking me what he could do.

I felt something I never had before—a complete loss of control. I couldn't manage my emotions. I couldn't make the worry or fear stop. My thoughts were racing, and my heart raced even faster. I felt helpless and scared, and the longer it persisted, the more I was convinced that I was dying. Eventually, it subsided, but I felt like something was physically wrong with me. There was no way it was all in my head.

So, I made an appointment with a doctor who told me, very matter of factly, that I had experienced a panic attack. "A panic attack?" What the hell was that, and why in the world would I have one? My questions then evolved into, "Will this happen again? How long will it last? How can I prevent it?" The doctor gave me a generic response, "Everyone is different," and gave me a prescription for Xanax should I need it.

I didn't like taking medicine then and still don't, so I only used it if I was desperate. I also had some aches and pains, including severe abdominal pain, which the doctor told me was just a symptom of my newly developed anxiety. Not convinced, I searched for a new provider in hopes of ruling out any underlying physical ailment. I had suffered from this pain for a while, and it had officially become unbearable.

I could not accept that this was a result of a panic attack. In my pursuit to find answers, I found an outstanding osteopathic medical physician, Dr. Capobianco, (D.O.). Upon evaluating me, he determined I was suffering from some musculoskeletal issues before also catching that I had acute appendicitis. I was off for surgery—and just in the nick of time! My gut was not only hurting, but it had been right. Something was wrong, and thankfully, my new doctor caught it. Thank God.

Coincidentally, he also happened to be from the East Coast. We bonded quickly over our shared origins, the things we loved and missed about New York, and eventually, our similar philosophies, approaches to life, health, and the persistent pursuit of peace. I got to know his family well and even babysat for them on occasions. Kind and compassionate, he shared his personal experience with anxiety during stressful times in medical school, making me feel a lot better.

I thought, if it could happen to a successful doctor, I wasn't alone, and there was hope for me. Once I recovered from my appendectomy, I was determined to overcome these bouts of panic and take better control of my health. I was fortunate to have found an excellent doctor who put me back together again through diet, supplements, natural medicine, and osteopathic manipulation. He also cared for my emotional wellbeing with genuine care and concern and became a lifelong friend.

Outside these lifestyle changes, I attended a few therapy sessions. I learned that anxiety can stem from something your subconscious is aware of, but your mind is either repressing or not allowing it to come to the surface. It's a general feeling of threat that you can't exactly pinpoint, but your brain is aware or believes danger exists, so your body goes into fight or flight mode. Anxiety and panic then begin to manifest.

Throughout these few sessions, the therapist would ask me how things were going in my life and if anything was troubling me. She went down the list: school, work, social life. "All fine," I said after each inquiry. Then, she asked me if everything was going well in my marriage, to which I replied, "Oh, yes! My marriage is great. My husband is wonderful, attentive, and we are so in love."

"Well then," she said, "there must be something else going on."

I was determined to get to the bottom of this mystery, cure myself, and prevent any more of the dreaded attacks.

Days after this conversation, I was walking up the stairs to our second-floor apartment and found a business card tucked in my door. The card read "Arlington Police Department, Detective Lewis," and just below his contact information, written in blue ink, was, "Call me."

I couldn't imagine why a detective would want to speak to me and assumed he had mistakenly placed the card on the wrong door. Pants had already gone down to Florida to report for spring training, while I stayed behind to finish up a few final exams. I had a lot to do before leaving, but I was excited to make the trip down there to support him.

I called the police department and asked for Detective Lewis. After explaining that I found his card on my door, he began by introducing himself and asked if my husband was around. He said it was essential that he speak to him right away. I inquired what it was about, but he said he couldn't give me any information other than that it pertained to his arrest.

"Arrest? What arrest?" I said. Further conveying that he could not share any details with me about the case, he kindly asked if I would have Pants give him a call. In just a few short minutes, the abbreviated phone conversation included the mention of an arrest and an ongoing case, and I was beside myself.

As I hung up the phone, all the familiar feelings of panic started to come over me like a giant, unavoidable wave. I immediately phoned the team secretary and had Pants called in off the field, stating that it was vital that I speak to him right away.

When Pants finally got on the phone, I frantically blurted out, "What the hell is going on?" Completely caught off guard, "What?" was all he said.

I went on. "You tell me. A detective Lewis called. Ring a bell?" He sputtered and laughed as he responded, "What are you talking about? Is this a joke?"

Growing impatient and even more frustrated, I shouted fearfully, "He said he needed to speak to you about your arrest! What is he talking about?" There was surprise in his voice after a slight delay, followed by "OMG! Those guys! My team is obviously playing a joke on me."

I wasn't convinced. I persisted, "How is that a joke? That's not even funny!"

Adamantly, he responded that it was "nothing" or maybe, as he suggested, "It could just be for some unpaid parking tickets on campus."

Feeling slightly relieved by his reassurance that it was either just a bad joke or a misunderstanding, I wanted to believe him. "Don't worry. I'll take care of it. It's nothing to worry about," he assured me. "I'll see you in a couple of weeks. Love you," he said.

I hung up the phone with mixed feelings but convinced myself that everything was (or would be) fine.

The next day, the detective called me back and asked if I could give him Pants' telephone number in Florida. He confirmed that he had spoken to him the day before but still had more questions for him and didn't get his number. When I asked what it was regarding, I was sure to mention that Pants told me that it must have been a joke that his teammates were playing on him and that I shouldn't worry. Detective Lewis firmly said, "It's not a joke."

Growing more and more scared, I pressed him, nearly begging for information, but he continued to say that he couldn't share any details with me. I got off the phone and sank to the floor. As I sat in the middle of my empty living room, I felt a terrible doom. Something was wrong.

I decided to drive to the police station and ask to see the detective in person. I had hoped that if I were standing in front of Detective Lewis, somehow, I could get more information from him. I don't know if it was seeing me, a young girl whose life he had a chance to spare, that he inevitably made him change his mind or something else. He invited me back to his office and began to tell me what Pants had hidden from me for many months.

He began by showing me some "booking" pictures and asking me to confirm that they were my husband. Shocked at what I was seeing, I tearfully said, "Yes, that's him." He let me listen to a recorded interview of Pants being questioned and testifying about his actions.

Unbeknownst to me, he had a big problem that he kept hidden, and I was blown away by the discovery. I learned that he had been arrested numerous times on campus for exposing himself to female students. The detective said Pants would habitually park near a girl studying in her car or resting before class, pull up next to her without his pants on, and expose himself. The information he shared with me was coming at a rate too fast for my mind to comprehend.

I felt like I was going to be sick. This nightmare wasn't my life. It couldn't be happening! Working full-time throughout college, I took several night classes with instructors who advised girls to walk out together because there was a "predator" hanging around campus. Campus security had issued warnings of someone performing indecent acts, so we were all aware of the safety of walking together, choosing well-lit walkways, and reporting any suspicious behavior.

How did I not know that my boyfriend, now my husband, was this disgusting person? I was married to a PREDATOR! This handsome, young, all-American baseball player had a rap sheet and charges that he carefully and craftily hid from me. I felt my world closing in and couldn't believe what I was hearing.

After seeing several of his mug shots, the detective informed me that Pants was being questioned for something more serious. *MORE SERIOUS*? *What could possibly be more serious than this?* I thought.

The place I'd lived previously quickly became a subject of interest to the detective, and I didn't understand why. When I first moved to Texas, I rented a studio apartment in a gated community called Peachtree-Peartree Apartments. While I still worked at the on-campus housing development, which was the company that transferred me from Oklahoma, I chose to forgo the free apartment offered to me as part of my compensation in exchange for a larger salary I desperately needed.

I'd found that I was able to save a little money living off-campus. After meeting Pants and later marrying, we moved into a larger one-bedroom apartment in the same complex but in a different building. Pants didn't live there long because his team had signed him on and would soon be heading off to Florida. I moved out shortly afterward.

After I moved out, horrific events had rocked the community. Two young women who had studied to be teachers, as I was, were murdered in their apartments within three months of each other while living in this same community. Both were raped and found strangled in their bathtubs. The detective told me the evidence pointed to a young, likely approachable, possibly athletic guy, who may have been familiar with the property since there was no sign of forced entry.

The investigation was now all over the news, exploring every possible theory, including that the killer may have been a good-looking and convincing guy who might have been invited in. There were too many correlations for the police to overlook. I studied to be a teacher and lived in this development with him previously, where two teachers were murdered. Along with his sexual deviance, his newly uncovered record, seemingly double life, skill at hiding things, and now being questioned, I couldn't breathe.

The detective shared with me that Pants had not only been arrested for indecent behavior on campus but had been caught driving and exposing himself to women at red lights. Then, there was the time he was staying at a hotel with other players and forced a girl to watch him masturbate. The stories all started to come out—even from a long-time friend who later shared with me that she caught him watching porn, and while that alone didn't alarm her, a feeling she had did.

I felt like my world was crumbling around me, and I didn't know what to do. It was a terrible nightmare from which I desperately wanted to wake. *Was this really happening? Was this my life? How could this be the guy I lived with and had dreamed of having a family with one day? How could he have hidden ALL of this from me? How did I not know?*

My "marriage" was annulled by the state and later by the church, ruling that he entered into the marriage under false pretenses and was not who he said he was. The only record of this terrible experience, up until now, would be lost and exist only in my mind as an awful memory. Until now, this chapter of my life has been locked up and stored away, never to see the light.

While I chose to bury this period of my life because of the pain, uncertainty, fear, loss of control, and the change in direction it brought into my life, I recognize that this trial served a purpose. I learned more about myself, my faith, and my determination to survive and succeed. It is only appropriate that I recognize and accept that this experience helped deliver me to a whole new level of enlightenment.

When things ended, I discovered that Pants had collected the mail every day because it contained dirty magazines. There were phone bills listing hundreds of dollars worth of 1-900 calls that Pants made while I was working and sleeping, and legal notices that he carefully kept from me.

With a truck I hated and a monthly payment that became my responsibility, I moved on with my life. Due to insufficient evidence, the murders of those two girls remained unsolved for years, and it haunted me. I often wondered if God had spared me from something much, much worse. Almost four years later, detectives discovered evidence leading to the case's closure and the death penalty of a suspected criminal. Pants was off the hook, and the issue had been solved and officially closed.

My negative experiences with men over the years created a strong distrust within me, and I would never again ignore my intuition and gut feelings. Knowing it was an unfair assumption to believe that all men were the same, I still kept my guard up and was never again one to have a naïve view of the world or the people in it. . . especially men.

Play Track 15 (Stop Draggin' My Heart Around – Stevie Nicks and Tom Petty) in Broken Little Believer Playlist

Baggage Check:

Has there ever been a time you've carried someone else's luggage, and the weight of it became unbearable? Have you been able to put it down and let it go?

Have you ever mistaken someone else's luggage as your own?

_____

_____

_____

_____

_____

_____

_____

_____

_____

_____

CHAPTER 16

Wildflowers

While finishing my degree and still working in the student housing community, I met Azhar. He was kind, thoughtful, and considerate. My first interaction with Azhar was after he attempted to show off in front of the window where my desk overlooked the front gate area. Trying to look cool and perform a stunt on his motorcycle, he failed miserably but did succeed at making me laugh—once I knew he was okay.

With an endearing disposition and a zest for life, I quickly understood why those closest to him referred to him as "Joy." Genuine in his mannerisms and direct with his actions, he had a trusted mysterious side that told me he was not your average college student. Beneath his smiling confidence, he knew struggle and hardship.

A mutual friend of ours tried to convince me to go out with him, but I wasn't ready to date. "Are you sure, Shane? He's a real catch!" I was sure. I didn't feel prepared for a romantic relationship, but I was open to being friends. Over the next few months, we would grab food, go for drives, and

I would even watch him as he competed in Motorcross races. He loved to push the envelope, go fast, and take risks. It was exhilarating, and I enjoyed his energy and enthusiasm. "Live life to the fullest" wasn't just a motto but an invitation he continually extended to me.

No matter what we did together, we had fun and enjoyed each other's company. As Azhar began to develop feelings for me, I struggled to understand what I felt. He would have given me the world, and he tried to, but I was still in a state of confusion and hurt over what had happened, and I resented anyone, especially a man, who tried to infringe upon my freedom or independence.

A "princely" man, Azhar was a guy my mother thought would give me the life I deserved. She commented on how "tall, dark, and handsome" he was. Her observations then pointed to how distinguished and intelligent he was. Azhar and I traveled to meet each other's families and supported one another as we worked toward our careers and future plans. I cared for Azhar deeply and felt a genuine love between us, but at times, the pain of all that I had gone through prevented me from truly appreciating him.

Azhar placed me on a pedestal and taught me what it meant to be cared for truly, but I pushed back when he asked me to commit. There was a certain insistency about him which I believe was a leadership quality that, at the time, felt more like a stifling of my spirit, and it made me want to run. And run, I did, and when he ran after me, I often regretted how I treated him.

My mixed reactions to his charm and determination to give me a beautiful life were sometimes to embrace it and others, to resist it. This ambivalence was an extension of my pain and fear of losing myself again. I indeed discovered *joy* in my relationship with him, but the time and circumstances were just not right.

After graduating from college, I taught school for a while. I loved it, but I had student loans to pay off and took a second temporary job which turned into a successful sales career. My mother had been urging me to come back to the East Coast for many years, and now that I had graduated, I found myself at a crossroads. Eventually, I realized there was no reason to remain in Texas and now was as good a time as any to move back. A new beginning was in order.

Play Track 16 (Wildflowers – Tom Petty) in Broken Little Believer Playlist

Baggage Check:

Has your "baggage" ever gotten in the way of a relationship? Perhaps your behavior, reactions, or interpretation of a particular experience was less than positive because of the luggage you brought into it?
Are you holding onto feelings of sorrow or regret because of how you treated someone?
Do you find it difficult to unpack or let go?

_____

_____

_____

_____

_____

_____

_____

_____

_____

_____

_____

SECTION 4

The Long Way Back (Chapters 17-25)

The Long Way Back is a section about reflection, enlightenment, and acceptance. It's a collection of many "aha moments" and proof of silver linings. This section shows how learning to bend with the road is a lifelong practice that brings peace and purpose to your journey if you learn to slow down and travel with passion, wonder, and conviction.

The Long Way Back is about overcoming hardships, loss, and sorrow yet seeing the beauty that exists within them. It's knowing that plans change, but we become who we are meant to be by embracing change.

This section is a testimony of personal growth and self-realization. It's a summary of all that we learn (the pretty and the painful parts) and how brokenness doesn't have to stop us from believing, achieving, and arriving at our desired destination.

CHAPTER 17

Oh, How the Years Go By

Upon returning to the East Coast, my mother and I had to get to know each other all over again. I was just a young girl who had to follow her rules when I last lived in New York. Now a woman myself, I was unfamiliar with her and she with me, and our relationship felt awkward. To say we hit some rough patches would be a vast understatement.

As the comfort level between us returned and old habits resurfaced, I remembered why I accepted the invitation to go to Nebraska that summer before high school. While I had gone off and grown in many ways, her unhappiness remained. She created a successful business and was doing well professionally—something for which I always gave her a lot of credit. Extremely resourceful and someone who never gives up or backs down, she always finds a way.

Personally, though, she was back to being single and even more set in her ways. When she became angry or upset and directed her hurtful words toward me, I could now get up and walk away. I didn't have to accept that kind of treatment anymore. We went through countless periods of not talking for weeks, sometimes months at a time, but over the years, these growing pains served to bring me greater clarity as I became more determined to set boundaries of my own.

As an adult, I recognized even more that my mother was a prisoner of her past. She couldn't let go of the pain. It haunted and held her down like shackles, interfering with her present and compromising her future. With never-ending gratitude for my mom and respect for what she had been through and the sacrifices she made, I chose to focus on the positives and tried to minimize the negatives. I learned that I had to limit my exposure to her because her negative energy would envelop me. Toxic to me and my spirit, Mom's bitterness would suffocate me if I was around it enough.

Recognizing that we can't choose our parents or the environment we are born into, and not wanting to because I believe it is all part of our plan, I think we get to choose what we want to inherit, embrace, and foster, as well as what we reject, change, and learn from. I knew what patterns and behaviors I didn't want to repeat, and I knew those I desired to draw from, nurture, and accentuate.

The rocky relationship I had with my mom was one I never took for granted, but I had to accept that it was inconsistent and often unhealthy. I felt blessed to maintain nurturing relationships with other people in my life. Through the years and across many states, my former middle school principal and I remained in touch. Before the days of email and cell phones, we wrote letters. No longer a student, I called Mr. Kane by his first name, Tom, as he and I continued to fill each other in on various happenings and exchange updates on our families. I enjoyed hearing about what his wife Barbara was up to, and of course, recaps of all the exciting adventures they were having together.

Tom was always concerned about me and would often remind me to take some time to relax and do things I enjoyed. Persistent in wanting to know how I *truly* was, he checked in with me regularly and always made it a point to tell me how proud he was of me and all that I had done with my life. Even if it was hundreds of miles away, I took comfort in his presence and found his consistent and reliable messages of care, concern, and support to be an unexpected blessing and a gift.

We had a unique and special bond, and while we didn't share biological genes, we did share a lot of similarities. Both Irish, we possessed a certain strong-headedness and disciplined determination. Faith-filled and eager to help in humanitarian ways, we also shared a love of writing and were diligent in staying in touch with those we cared for.

Our letter writing, beginning just after I moved to Nebraska, always included a special message from him. His signature, "TSC of YSS, Tom," stood for "Take Special Care of Your Special Self." I read those six letters on every single communication, card, and email we exchanged for over thirty years. Soon, three more letters would be added to our special closing message, while another change would make it even more meaningful.

When I moved back, we picked up right where we left off. Reminiscent of earlier days, we often had lunch together—only now the food was better. We had graduated from cafeteria tray food to some of our favorite dishes at nearby trendy restaurants.

Play Track 17 (Oh How the Years Go By – Amy Grant) in Broken Little Believer Playlist

Baggage Check:

Do you recognize the gifts and the blessings that lost or misplaced luggage can sometimes represent? Can you think of a time in your life or an experience where you found peace in something that was lost, knowing that it didn't serve you anymore?

_____

_____

_____

_____

_____

_____

_____

_____

_____

_____

_____

_____

CHAPTER 18

I Knew You Were Waiting for Me

Living on my own in New York and New Jersey was an eye-opening experience. I missed small-town, USA quaintness, the country's openness, and the Midwest "Bless your heart" vibe. With a rushed pace and a cramped feel, the big city was overflowing with no-nonsense attitudes that felt cold and callused. It wasn't easy to get to know people in this area. Most kept their heads down on a determined mission-like state, and I couldn't help but notice a lack of eye contact and an absence of physical connection. Air kisses on the cheeks now took the place of the giant, rocking hugs I had become accustomed to out west.

On the professional side of things, I had moved up the ladder in sales and created a successful career for myself. I was traveling all over the country as a VP of Sales, making and saving good money and finding growing confidence in my abilities, various accomplishments, and continued independence.

At my age, and in the area where I lived, I had a lot going for me. I was a young, single, fiercely independent woman with a self-earned college degree, a successful career, a sparkly new car, my own apartment, and a growing savings account. I was in no rush to settle down, and I was not looking for, nor did I need, a man to take care of me.

While it is customary to smile at people in the Midwest, I quickly discovered that smiling at someone on the East Coast could be interpreted as you "like them." I was not prepared for the attention or love interest that was coming my way, and it seemed the more uninterested in a relationship I was, the more guys were intrigued.

Of course, the attention was a boon to my self-esteem, but I found myself turned off by the immaturity of many and the "Badda Bing, Badda Boom" mentality of some others. I began to feel like I had made a mistake moving back. It seemed I had traded living in an area where people still hailed old-fashioned manners and respect for living in a congested area of the superficial, "So, what do you do for a living?" mentality. I focused on my career and resolved to believe that Mr. Right, who I felt was bound to be a cowboy, would come later in my life and certainly not in New Jersey.

I had just returned from a business trip to China when a friend called to invite me to a barbecue. Wearing lounge-around-the-house clothes and with my hair pulled back into a ponytail, I was jet-lagged, but my friend persisted and convinced me to "just come as you are."

It was there that I met Rich. I didn't know yet that he was Mr. Right, but subsequent dates uncovered a man who was not only tall, strong, and handsome, but funny, intelligent, respectful, sensitive, and compassionate too.

The middle child of three boys, he grew up working hard and learning how to do everything by hand. His father put the boys to work, and together, they gained experience and appreciation for building houses. The family also created functional and beautiful landscape designs, including stunning rock walls. They fixed vehicles, restored boats, and many other items.

Their father taught them to be disciplined and to take pride in their work. Exuding endless know-how and creativity and possessing an easy-going temperament he inherited from his mother, Rich impressed me with his diverse skill set. He allured me with his gentle demeanor and wowed me with his self-taught cooking and brewing abilities. Proud to be of Czechoslovakian heritage, Rich swept me off my feet.

We met each other's friends and families, and soon, I introduced Rich to Tom. Tom wanted to be sure that Rich was a good man and treated me well. He emphasized how important my happiness was and reminded me never to settle or compromise. He also made it clear to Rich that he was watching, although Rich made it very easy for him, and it didn't take long for Tom to rule that my boyfriend was a good guy.

The two hit it off splendidly, and the four of us, Rich, Tom, Barbara, and I, enjoyed many dinners and, together, attended various special celebrations. I can't quite pinpoint when or how it happened. Still, as my relationship with Tom continued to evolve over the years, it began to feel more like a father/daughter relationship—or at least it felt a lot like what I imagined a father/daughter relationship would be. I had a tremendous amount of respect and admiration for Tom, and I valued his thoughts and opinions more than any other.

At some point along the way, he added three new letters, LYL (love you lots), to his signature that filled my heart with a feeling that had long existed but had never been spoken. From that moment on, he signed everything, TSC of YSS and LYL, Dad.

Rich and I fell hard, and we fell fast—something that scared me a great deal. We both confessed our love to one another and our hopes for the future. Before moving forward, I wanted him to know all about me and my life, and I wanted to know everything about him, too. Did Rich have any dark secrets or skeletons hidden in his closet? Was there any well-disguised dysfunction or destructive addiction that I needed to know about? Was this man a hard worker I could depend upon to be a good father?

I didn't hold back sharing my list of non-negotiables with Rich and wanted to be sure that he understood and accepted these things. I didn't care about money or what kind of job he had, the car he drove, or what he could give me. I wanted to be sure he was a good, hard-working, God-fearing man who would be a devoted father to our children. I didn't think it was too much to ask for, and I had no reservations in making that clear.

We had many of the same interests: travel, health, fitness, spending time outdoors, live music, and country living. Although we grew up differently, we both learned the importance of hard work, responsibility, character, and integrity. The more time we spent together, the more I knew—*I have found the one whom my soul loves (Song of Solomon 3:4)*.

On September 11th, 2001, I was working in the city when our world stopped spinning, and our country changed forever. The World Trade Center was under terrorist attack, and the heinous acts left us and everyone watching, crippled in horror and disbelief. The two towers had been hit by commercial planes, and panic quickly spread up and down the streets as fear took hold of everyone. My company's showroom was just two floors below the rooftop, where we often enjoyed unobstructed views of the city, and now, direct visibility of the World Trade Center. High up in the sky, the building shook with fear and commotion.

Phone lines and other forms of communication were not functioning, and our country was in a state of shock and confusion. Rich, fearing where I was in relation to the towers, repeatedly tried to reach me by phone, but to no avail. With no way of calling each other and no way to get out of the city, we both felt helpless and scared. The slow-moving minutes turned into hours that quickly became a day of dread and dust. With nowhere to go and nothing to do but pray and wait, "the city that never sleeps" became an eerily quiet triage station. The sounds of sirens served as evidence of life and loss.

I was one of the lucky ones who made it across the bridge just as the brigade of flatbeds and heavy equipment (the only traffic coming in) filed in on the West Side Highway. It was a heartbreaking and horrific sight to witness, knowing the wreckage they were being called in to clear and haul away. Amidst the dust and dirt-stained faces, I could see trails of tears on the faces of those desperately trying to escape the horror and get home to their loved ones.

As much as I wanted to get out of the city, part of me wanted to stay. An indescribable and immeasurable feeling of human connection came over the country that day and in the weeks that followed, as people came together exhibiting more selflessness, resilience, and American pride than I had ever seen before.

Without saying a word, love was present and seen in the eyes of strangers. Everyone shared the same mixture of feelings: confusion over what was happening, fear of the unknown, love for one another and our country, and resolve to recover and overcome. It was a time when there was only one race in existence—the human race. This tragic event rocked our country to the core and reminded everyone of life's preciousness and fragility.

When I finally arrived back in New Jersey, where Rich anxiously waited for me, we rushed to each other in an embrace that was different than any other we had experienced before. We knew we wanted to be together forever, and this experience solidified who and what mattered most in our lives. Not long after, Rich went down on one knee and proposed to me on the ice-skating rink at Rockefeller Center. It was one of the happiest days of my life. It was only natural to ask Tom (aka Dad) to walk me down the aisle on my wedding day. Honored, he gladly accepted.

In preparation for the special day, I booked adjoining rooms at a nearby hotel for my bridesmaids and me to stay the night before. Not only did it provide us with some much-needed time together since all but two bridesmaids had flown in from other states, but it proved to be convenient for us all to get ready together the following morning.

I arranged for my hairdresser, along with a makeup artist, to come the morning of the wedding to assist me, my mom, and my bridal party, making us feel beautiful for my special day. My mother was upset because she didn't like her hair, makeup, or outfit, and everyone knew it.

We were running late and needed to get to the church. The limo was outside waiting for us, and my brother was nowhere to be found. I was certain Chris would go straight to the church since he had an invitation with the address, and I told Mom that we needed to leave as we were already late.

After everyone piled into the limo, she announced, "You know, it's always about you and what you want." And before I could say anything, one of my friends said, "Well, it is her wedding day." My mother's mood and the grimace on her face did not soften as she proceeded to express her unhappiness about everything.

It was a perfect September day, similar to the morning of the 9/11 attacks that had occurred only one year earlier. When we pulled up in front of the church we regularly attended, standing outside and awaiting my arrival, was my "dad" ready to help me out of the limo. The photographer captured an unscripted moment that will forever be a favorite memory of mine.

As Tom reached down to help me out of the limo, he kissed my hand and gave me his arm as I pulled my train from the car. In my face, you can see the sheer happiness I felt at that moment and the gratitude I felt for the special relationship that had developed over so many years. I'm confident that much of my mom's displeasure and unhappiness surrounding that day was because I had asked him to accompany me down the aisle, but I had my reasons. I didn't want anything to be as it had been before.

My brother and mother had that role once, and nothing about it was right. Still wanting to include her, I did ask her if she would walk on one side of me, and though she had agreed, it was clear she resented the relationship I had with Tom and felt my brother should have walked me down the aisle. I was happy with my decision, and I had no regrets. It was exactly as it should have been.

A special moment, now a priceless memory.

183

I understand why my mother behaved the way she did. I followed a different path. I was the first person in my family to earn a college degree, have a successful career, and fall in love with a good man who would not only be an excellent husband but a responsible father one day too. I didn't allow the absence of my natural father to be an excuse, but an example. I learned from it, and I let it go and discovered that while any man can be a father, it takes someone extraordinary to be a dad.

I suppose this is why I rationalized Mom's behavior and "turned the other cheek" when things went sour between us. I became keenly aware of and accustomed to her changing moods and tried my best to adjust how I responded to them. This coping mechanism would prove valuable to me later in life as I became adept at picking up on subtle energy changes. This skill allows me to assess situations and head off problems quickly before they escalate.

Play Track 18 (I Knew You Were Waiting (For Me) – George Michael & Aretha Franklin) in Broken Little Believer Playlist

Baggage Check:

When tragedy strikes, we find that our luggage and belongings are less critical than we originally supposed. It's during these events that we realize what matters and what doesn't.
Can you recall a time in your life or an experience you lived through that taught you what was most important?

_____

_____

_____

_____

_____

_____

_____

_____

_____

_____

CHAPTER 19

Piece by Piece

After honeymooning in Hawaii, Rich and I returned to New Jersey to begin our lives together as husband and wife. We bought a cute colonial home on a quiet street in a friendly neighborhood. Annual block parties consisted of music, fun, and tasty dishes of every ethnicity. Our neighborhood was a lot like the United Nations, and when we assembled, it was sure to be a good time. An authentic representation of allies, we helped one another, supported each other, and came together when someone needed something. We made incredible friends and cherished memories.

We knew we wanted to start a family right away and decided to allow God to bless us when the time was right. We traveled, had lots of fun, worked hard, made our house a home, welcomed a few pets, and said goodbye to some too. We were ready to have a baby, and I was concerned when it didn't happen right away. It had been a year since we were married, so I decided to make an appointment for us both to have a check-up to be sure everything was okay. It was, and there was no reason for us not to get pregnant; it just hadn't happened yet.

I began to track my fertility by recording my temperature and noting other hormonal changes, but still, nothing happened. The doctor called it "unexplained infertility" and said that it was relatively common. He suggested we start with a round or two of intrauterine insemination (IUI), which is less invasive than in-vitro fertilization (IVF), and see if that would do the trick.

I had just come home from a business trip in Ohio, and I was anticipating the call. We were on try number two of IUI, and I told myself not to get my hopes up. I said to myself that it would be negative to avoid too much disappointment. Rich was still at work when the phone rang.

"May I speak to Shane Svorec?" the woman on the other end asked, to which I casually replied, "This is Shane."

Without skipping a beat, she announced, "Your test was positive."

"Positive?" I questioned. "What do you mean it was positive?"

With little emotion and in a very matter-of-fact manner, she said, "Your HGH levels are elevated, so the test was positive." Wanting to hear her say those two magical words, I finally asked, "So, are you saying I'm pregnant?

I sensed she was annoyed when she finally said, "Yes, you're pregnant, but anything could happen. It's still early."

I suppose they make it a practice not to show much emotion because things can and do happen. I just remember saying, "REALLY? Are you sure?" over and over again, and then finally, "What do I do now?"

As soon as I hung up the phone, I dropped to my knees and thanked God for allowing me to conceive and experience this blessing. My life changed at that moment, and I made it my biggest priority to take care of the beautiful being growing inside me.

We were very excited expectant parents and had a lot of fun as we waited to meet our bundle of joy. I reveled in my pregnancy and documented every bit of it. I loved watching my belly grow and feeling my baby's tiny feet kick. I had a beautiful, uncomplicated pregnancy, although I probably ate too many cookies and milk, my delicious solution to the challenge of increasing my calcium. Rich never tired of walking our dog, Max, to the Dairy Queen around the corner and getting blizzards for us and a doggy cone for him. We ALL enjoyed my pregnancy.

We found out we were having a girl. I was terrified. All I could think of was my childhood, and I felt an overwhelming obligation and responsibility to protect her and not screw her up. When we began looking at baby names, we decided to sit down independently and list our favorites. When we came together to review our lists, Lainey was on both. Her name means "bright light" or "Heaven."

My mom threw me a beautiful, surprise baby shower at a restaurant near her house. She went there often, and the food was good. She had been in touch with several of my friends and made arrangements to pick one of them up from the airport the night before to surprise me. My friend, Nancy, told me afterward about her and my mom's "adventures," vowing never to surprise me again if it meant staying with my mom and going along with her plans.

After picking her up from the airport, they stopped at my mom's place, then went out to grab a bite to eat. They got food poisoning and were sick much of the night, but as they began to feel better, my mom said she wanted to drive my friend by the restaurant where my baby shower would be the next day. My friend admitted that she didn't feel like going. She still wasn't feeling great and was tired from the flight but thought she had no choice and went along for the ride.

It was late at night, and the restaurant was already closed. Nancy said, "As we drove over there, your mom told me how great the food was and how I would enjoy it much more than what we ate last night! But when we arrived, she saw the restaurant's front door and started to worry about how it looked and whether family and friends would get a bad impression. She became fixated on it and didn't like that the paint was peeling off."

Convinced, as my friend told me the story, that my mom was more concerned about what people thought of the restaurant SHE chose, what she told me next left me speechless but not surprised. While Nancy was tired and still not feeling well, my mom suggested they paint the door! Despite my friend's best efforts to convince her that it was okay as it was, my mom was determined to fix it.

She drove them to Home Depot, picked out a paint color, and together, they drove back to paint the restaurant's front door. It wasn't until they finished that Nancy considered and mentioned to my mom that the restaurant could have security cameras. What if they saw them there in the middle of the night? The fear of trespassing and possible vandalism charges began to build. They packed up the paint can and brushes and left in a hurry, wondering if the owners would notice or discover anything.

As my baby shower was winding down and I sat in the restaurant's upstairs party room, I gasped, laughed, and almost peed myself as my friend secretly told me the story. Of course, when I left, I looked long and hard at the front door and will forever think of my mom and her unwilling accomplice when I hear the first lines of the song Paint It Black. I knew my mom meant well (she has a big heart), but she is the whackiest person I know, and her judgment and methods are a bit unconventional.

"Bright Light, Heaven" could not have been a more accurate description when I looked into the wide-eyed, beautiful soul who entered our world two weeks past her due date. She captured my heart with one look, and in her expression, I could discern wisdom that stretched far beyond her new life. With her big eyes staring back at me, she reached deep into my soul as I spoke to her. All I could say was, "I've waited a long time to meet you, Lainey. I'm your mommy." I cried such happy tears that day and felt a love like I had never known.

She was glued to me from the start. She hated sleeping in her crib, so I often brought her to bed to fall asleep with me. Even our dog, Max, a rescued pit bull and a new member of the family himself, with a "chocolate chip nose" and green eyes, loved Lainey. He guarded her crib when we tried to get her to sleep in it and would lie next to her when she was on her playmat or in her Exersaucer.

Wherever Lainey was, Max was there too. They seemed to comprehend and have a special relationship. Lainey grew up with Max. The two were inseparable, understanding one another and demonstrating a love that few understand between a child and their pet, Max being a breed that many misunderstood to boot. We have always taught our children that love knows no boundaries, exceptions, or limits. How we treat and care for others is a direct representation of our hearts, not theirs.

We enjoyed life as parents and had fun with our many "firsts." Not long after Lainey turned one, we found out that we were expecting again....and all on our own! We never imagined that it would happen so readily or without assistance. We thought we might have to plan our pregnancy again. It turns out my body just needed a little jump start but was now ready to prove itself.

Our second baby was a BOY! We couldn't have been more excited! This event is where my story comes full circle, and I decided (with Rich's approval) that he should be named Jack after my grandfather. Jack Richard is a bold name for a strong boy. I had another easy pregnancy, thank God, and ate fewer cookies with milk this time.

Unlike his sister, Jack was born two weeks early. My pregnancy and birth were documented on the TV show "A Baby Story." The greatest gift to come out of this experience was that it captured my grandparents' importance in my life. It showcased a clip of my grandmother rubbing my pregnant belly, a memory I will always have, thanks to that filming.

Jack was a super happy, easy baby. He was excitable and energetic and always full of smiles and drool. He slept like a champ in his crib and never complained. What a joyful boy! Lainey and Jack were very close, and Lainey always looked out for Jack. She still does. They cherish and care for each other and enjoy a closeness that I simply adore.

Having children of my own, I experienced love like never before. My life was richer and more meaningful because of immeasurable joy, hope, pride, fear, and a sense of near-Herculean protection. Their safety, happiness, and well-being became my number one priority. I couldn't imagine being separated from either one of them.

As I look back on my life and childhood, I feel I love my children even more because of it. Surrounded by dysfunctional communication styles and having learned to accept rationed disbursements of affection, a mission of mine as a mother is to encourage speaking honestly, loving freely, and giving generously.

Play Track 19 (Piece by Piece (Idol Version)– Kelly Clarkson) in Broken Little Believer Playlist

Baggage Check:

Can you relate to all of the emotions that go along with carrying precious cargo? The feeling of wanting to protect it at all costs? Could that cargo could be a child, a pet, or another loved one?

_____

_____

_____

_____

_____

_____

_____

_____

_____

_____

_____

_____

CHAPTER 20

Have a Little Faith in Me

Life was good, and my heart was full! Before we married, like most couples, we talked about how many kids we wanted to have. Two or three was the consensus, but I told Rich that I had always wanted to foster. I was fortunate to find a man who believed in and supported me and my hopes, dreams, and aspirations. As our children grew, we talked about the idea of having a third, and I reminded him of my wish to foster one day.

Since twins run on both sides of our families, Rich was convinced that we could very well end up with four if we decided to have a third child. This prospect did not deter me at all, but welcoming more children into our family was a consideration that we wanted to discuss thoroughly. We both felt incredibly blessed to have two healthy children, and when our children were a little older, we moved into a bigger home and prepared to open our hearts and home to other children who needed it.

Ever since I was a little girl, I knew I wanted to help children. When bad things happened to me, I told myself that there had been a reason, a purpose, for why I faced the things I did, and I believed my ability to understand and relate to others was part of it. It felt important that we open our children's eyes to what some kids don't have that we can provide.

Excited by the idea of helping other children, our kids were on board with fostering. We knew it wouldn't be easy, and we did our best to help them understand the challenges and sacrifices of this decision, including sharing their home, belongings, and parents with others. There really is no way to prepare yourself or your family for this kind of journey, though.

We would all discover that every call, every child, and every placement, presented different circumstances and challenges. Fostering children is often disheartening, disturbing, disappointing, and scary, but it is also rewarding, fulfilling, and promising. With each goodbye and many degrees of heartache, I found that my heart could regenerate and create renewed and restored supplies of love. It could mend what broke, pave a new way, and make space for more love.

We have loved and cared for over eleven children through the years. Some were temporary or emergency placements, while others were long-term. Our very first placement was a newborn baby girl who stayed with us for almost a year. I fell in love with her. We all did. Her birth name, referring to an astronomical event, felt appropriate as she became a bright but temporary star in our home, though forever present in our hearts.

Fortunate to have also cared for her brother when he was born a year later, we became close with the distant family members, who were eventually granted placement and adoption of them both. It was a painful but beautiful experience that brought two loving families together out of shared love and commitment to the care of these children. I am blessed to remain in contact with them to this day and grateful to have been part of their beginnings. While we were sad to say goodbye, we were happy they went to a good home where they would be loved and protected.

We added a third child to our permanent family who came to us through fostering, and we ultimately adopted. She was my "Destiny" and challenged everything I knew and believed. Resilient, outgoing, funny, and clever, she added action to our family with her bubbly, bright, never-still energy level. Stubborn beyond stubborn, she gave me a run for my money, and I pushed her to be all that she could be—even when she didn't feel like it. My greatest fear for her was a lack of ambition.

She is capable, intelligent, and resourceful. Still, I worried that she depended too much on others to do things for her and became comfortable asking. As a parent, my obligation and goal were to teach her independence, confidence, and self-reliance. Parenting is one of the most complex jobs in the world, but it is also one of the most gratifying and fulfilling.

With different personalities, strengths, weaknesses, likes, and dislikes, I have tried hard to foster our children's uniqueness while instilling within them the knowledge that their differences make them special. With plenty of love, support, and boundaries, if my children learn nothing else, I hope and pray they realize that success and happiness are not guaranteed—they both require consistent commitment and conscious cultivation. We are responsible for our own success and joy, and we hold the keys to both of them if we genuinely want to achieve them.

I believe in my children and love them more than life itself. It won't be an endless supply of money, fancy cars, or the enrollment in elite schools, but principles of honesty, hard work, and examples of character and integrity that we strive to give them to promote their happiness and future success.

Fostering children has been one of the most rewarding and challenging experiences I've faced. Many times I felt court-appointed representatives and judges failed the children for whom I loved and cared. There were other times I was reassured and relieved by their decisions.

No matter what the circumstances were for a child's removal, I couldn't help but feel *some* sense of sadness for their biological parents. Despite this compassion that I felt for them, I learned very early that my heart could only carry so much pain and responsibility in our fostering journey. My job was to care for and love the children. But I could pray for their parents.

Fostering gave me a feeling of fulfillment as part of my purpose. It allowed me to answer the calls of families in need while listening to, understanding, and advocating for those without a voice. With a fierce protective streak, I found it easy to stand up and speak out for those who had been neglected or pushed around. My goal was to give back some of what I had, add more, and take less from this world. More than just hearing what people had to say, I wanted to listen and understand them. I tried to use my past pain for a positive purpose by appreciating all that I had been given and share what I could with others.

It was Christmastime in 2017, and I shopped for gifts, recreated some of our favorite traditions, and made new ones with my children. Like many holidays before, I thought back to times when I had nowhere to go, and holidays were a lonely time. When other college students went home for the holidays, I stayed behind in my dorm or apartment. I was fortunate and grateful to receive invitations from friends or classmates to join them for a family dinner or get-together.

I recall going to a friend's house for Thanksgiving, and another friend's for Christmas. Other times, people I knew would bring dishes or treats back to share with me on occasions like Easter. The holidays stirred up memories, and while many were nostalgic of fun times at Memie and Boppie's, some brought back memories of sad, lonely times.

With Christmas music playing in the background, twinkling lights, and holiday decorations creating a warm and inviting space with picturesque views, my kids were busy making their wish lists for Santa. Everything was beautiful and nearly perfect, but I couldn't help feeling like something was missing.

While I received calls for children of all ages needing placement, I often wondered about those over eighteen who aged out of foster care or were never adopted. Many people don't realize that while children can be placed in a foster home at any age, it doesn't mean that a family will adopt them. Therefore, a child can be fostered until the age of eighteen, but technically, not ever have a family or a place they feel comfortable calling "home." I knew a need existed, but many, unless they had a personal experience such as mine, were unaware of it.

At Christmastime in 2017, I felt like everything in my life had come full circle. I had inquired before about adolescents who might not have a place to go for the holidays, but now I was undeterred in my mission to find them and give them a place to go. For over a year, resource workers told me they would "look into it." I didn't fault them for procrastinating because state workers are SO overworked, and there's not enough time in the day to meet the overwhelming needs. But now, I needed answers.

Where are the kids people haven't adopted? Where do they go, or who do they call when they are having a tough time or need a shoulder to cry on? Where do they go for the holidays if they don't have any family? If a young person in their position was fortunate enough to go to college, where do they go during the breaks?

As someone who had been out on my own at an early age and having no real "home base," I was aware of this need and familiar with this type of displacement and uncertainty. I had felt like a misfit before and lacked a sense of belonging. I spent many holidays with families of classmates, neighbors, and even kind strangers—a friend of a friend who was kind enough to allow an extra guest at the table.

I understood the "misfit club," and I felt compelled to help when, and how, I could. It became an unspoken vow early in life that I would return the favor one day and provide that welcoming home and warm meal for someone else. I don't know if I recognized the need in others or if others saw familiarity in me or shared commonality. Still, it was a natural and regular occurrence for me to have people over for dinners, holidays, and other occasions.

It was always a vibrant assembly consisting of colleagues from work, a single friend, or a lonely neighbor or two, which became some of my favorite memories at my mixed holiday gatherings. That was, until Christmas 2017. After trying so long to reach teens, whom I believed to be the most often overlooked, the state forwarded my invitation to the adolescent division. It read as follows:

Hello, Division of Youth Team,

As a follow-up to our phone conversation, I have inquired several times about children who may not have a place to go for Christmas.

Perhaps it's a child who has aged out of foster care, or one who lives alone, is away at college, or simply has no home base. I am not looking to be compensated. I am simply offering a warm and loving home to spend the holidays.

I would be interested in having one (or several) youth, come to our home to spend Christmas, enjoy a home-cooked meal and gifts.

Please let me know if this opportunity exists. I'm sure there are children out there who need a place to go.
Sincerely,
Shane Svorec
Resource Parent

With limited staff and insufficient resources available to dedicate to this type of unprecedented program, it seemed another holiday would go by without me filling this need that I knew existed. About a week after I sent the email, I received a follow-up call informing me that while they appreciated the offer, they ran out of time and believed that most of their adolescents had found a place to go. They said that going forward, they would be sure to share my invitation much sooner in hopes of reaching these teens for subsequent holidays if my offer was still open. "Of course," I replied, but I was disappointed that I couldn't see this intention of mine become a reality. I had no choice but to continue with my usual holiday planning and preparations.

The Thursday before Christmas, I received a call from my resource worker informing me that they found a nineteen-year-old boy named Michael who had nowhere to go. He stayed with a friend and his family, but the family was going away for the holiday. There was much more to his story, and the more she shared with me about Michael and his background, the more I knew he belonged with us.

I asked her to give Michael my cell phone number in case he wanted to text me and get to know me a little before Christmas. He did, and we quickly formed a bond even before we met. I was excited to shop for him, and in our texts, I found ways to get an idea of what he liked so that I could make Christmas a little more special and memorable for him. I could tell that he was happy to have been invited, and he continued by thanking me for giving him "something to look forward to." Oh, how my heart felt a familiar beat.

To my surprise, I received a second call the day before Christmas Eve about another teen boy who had nowhere to go. Darius was all packed up and already en route to a distant relative's house to spend Christmas when the worker driving him received a phone call informing her not to bring Darius because "something came up" and they wouldn't be able to have him after all.

Just days before Christmas, Darius was devastated. I came to learn that this was not the first time his relative had done this to him and canceled at the last minute. Darius's response to his caseworker as she turned the car around was, "I had a feeling this would happen." My heart broke for him. I was thrilled to extend the invitation to him as well. With just a day to shop for him, I asked the caseworker what Darius's interests were, and all she could tell me was that he once mentioned wanting a hockey jersey.

When the caseworker asked Darius what team he liked, he responded, "I don't care. I just want a hockey jersey." So, I crossed my fingers and picked a team, along with a few other gifts. They sat under the tree, wrapped with their names on them, waiting to be opened. Our kids were excited to hear they were joining us and couldn't wait to meet them. They decided that they would also do something special for them and made personalized ornaments for them—each one sweeter and more meaningful than the next.

Christmas morning arrived, and the kids opened their gifts from Santa before I put the turkey in the oven. Not long after, the doorbell rang, and excitement bubbled over everyone in the house as the kids yelled, "They're here!" The driver, a transporter for the state I already knew from previous other children in my care, dropped them off and said she planned to pick them up later that night.

After welcoming them in and exchanging hellos, I introduced Michael and Darius to my family and our pets. They were both much taller than I had imagined, and as I watched them look around and take in their surroundings, I could sense the initial awkwardness I'd always felt when I went to an unfamiliar home.

I kept the atmosphere and conversation light and told the boys to make themselves comfortable. "Our home is your home, so help yourself," I said. Michael and Darius were slightly bashful at first, but once I set out some appetizers, gave them each a soda, and told them to go watch whatever they wanted on TV or help themselves to the Xbox, they were at ease, and I could almost feel them exhale, which made me breathe easier too.

Our family spent the day talking with our guests about music, sports, school, places we'd lived, places we want to visit, possible jobs and career choices, and of course, what food was coming out next. I would catch myself smiling while cooking or cleaning throughout the day, and I thoroughly enjoyed watching Michael and Darius take second and third helpings. It made my heart happy to see them well fed, feeling comfortable, laughing, and having fun.

When they opened their gifts, I saw excitement and joy in their eyes. THIS was my favorite part. It brought me happiness that even I can't put into words. While Michael ripped the wrapping paper and tore into the boxes, Darius was slow and intentional. He took his time opening his gifts as if savoring every second. He reminded me of myself, and I was overjoyed to have this opportunity.

As I watched our children look on as the boys opened their gifts, I could see their excitement too. They had beaming expressions of curiosity on their faces as they closely watched Michael and Darius' reactions to see if they liked the things we picked out.

My favorite was when Darius opened the box with the hockey jersey inside. His eyes lit up as I've never seen from a teen as he audibly gasped and said, "Oh my gosh!" in surprise. I couldn't hold it in any longer and had to ask him if he liked it, was the team ok, did I get the right size, to which he replied, "Oh, yes!"

We spent the day eating, laughing, and then eating some more. We played a game similar to charades, and as we all laughed hysterically, I reveled in the boys' relaxed and comfortable state. THIS day was my definition of a Merry Christmas. It was what I had always dreamed of, and I wanted to do more.

The phone rang around six pm, and the transporter asked what time she should pick up the boys. I asked them what time they wanted to leave, and they both responded, "We will stay as late as you'll let us."

I didn't have to ask them if they had fun or enjoyed Christmas with us; they already said it in their response. The worker suggested 7:30 since she had to drive quite a distance to bring them both to their separate homes and get back to hers, so we settled on that.

Before they left, we took a few pictures, exchanged more numbers, and I told them that we had one more important rule in our home. As anxiousness quickly appeared on their faces, I announced, "Once you come to our home, you are always welcome back." This was the best, most fulfilling, heartwarming Christmas I'd ever had.

We continued to welcome teens to our home for the holidays, and the group grew over the years. Some have drifted, while some continue to call and stay in touch. Whether we shared one holiday or frequent, ongoing get-togethers, every teen matters, and we remember every visit. There have been many lunches, countless day trips, assistance with job interviews, conversations regarding school advice, best cars to purchase, and, of course, dating. Since their first Christmas invitation, knowing they had someone to turn to for these things made me happy.

On Valentine's Day, February 14, 2018, I received a call informing me that I was chosen as Foster Parent of the month. I wasn't even aware this award existed, and I was overwhelmed. I was recognized for fostering and spearheading an initiative to reach teens and adolescents who aged out of the system. They shared with me that the boys still had not stopped talking about Christmas at the Svorecs, and they could now see how much this service is needed and the difference it makes. Twenty-six years earlier, I received a letter from the foster parent division of the state of Nebraska recognizing me for my efforts as a young leader who had overcome my circumstances, and now, I was receiving recognition as a foster parent myself.

This honor was no ordinary award to me. It was a reminder of how far I had come, a testament of my will to thrive, then and now. It confirmed what I always knew: that everyone needs someone to believe in them, someone who sees something special even when they don't— to know that people are in their corner rooting for them and pushing them to get back up. This award reminded me that I was that boxer, refusing to stay down and relentlessly getting back up. Now, I was in the corner rooting for others who needed it.

These are moments where dignity, compassion, and humanity come shining through someone who has known pain, suffering, and loneliness. We choose to learn from those experiences rather than ignore them and try to be friends with another person struggling. The lessons these experiences imparted to our children were compassion, resilience, and conviction—qualities that will carry them forward in this world.

Play Track 20 (Have a Little Faith in Me – Joe Cocker) in Broken Little Believer Playlist

Baggage Check:

Can you recall a time when you shared the contents of your luggage with someone else? Have you experienced, or can you recognize, the feeling of fulfillment and satisfaction of sharing your belongings or your heart with another?

_____

_____

_____

_____

_____

_____

_____

_____

_____

_____

_____

_____

CHAPTER 21

The House That Built Me

The world was changing, but it didn't feel like a positive adjustment. As we became busier and busier, it seemed like humanity was becoming lost. I found that living on the East Coast exaggerated these feelings within me, and I craved change. I needed to remember who I was, where I came from, and what I needed and wanted in life.

I had spent years trying to create a positive and purposeful life, but I felt something was missing. Was it the hectic lifestyle of New Jersey? Or had I seen and felt too much? I struggled with this feeling of needing to fulfill my purpose, and although my husband often said that I was living it, I still thought there was something else, something more, that I was meant to do or accomplish. I did know that the longer I remained in one place, the more I felt stuck.

My awareness of people and the world around me was at an all-time high. I became discouraged by the changes I saw—the lack of respect, accountability, gratitude, and an increase in feelings of entitlement. Many seemed to have lost perspective, but I was bound to keep mine in check.

It became harder and harder to do as people gave excuses to explain away lousy behavior and poor examples of character and integrity. I needed to revisit places and remember people who helped shape me. I needed to hold onto my faith and keep looking up. Despite my fear and disappointments in what I perceived to be happening in the world, I was resolved and even more determined to hold onto my convictions and fulfill my desire to make a difference. At the very least, I did not want the world to change me; I tried to change the world, or at least a small part of it. Soon, I became known as "The Look Up Girl," and people followed me for encouragement.

"The Journey Home, A Project of the Heart" became the name of my pilgrimage back to memorable places that left an imprint on my heart. For me, "home" meant many places and many things, so the journey was not just about visiting one destination or doing so during one time period. Instead, it happened over a string of times, places, and experiences.

Revisiting places gave me a different perspective. It allowed me to find peace and purpose in the painful memories, and it reminded me of the beautiful ones I carry with me and still cherish today. Going back, literally or figuratively, I would find the person I was and remind her of the girl who still existed within me. At times, I felt like she needed to be embraced, encouraged, and empowered to continue to follow her heart and realize her dreams. Some places brought back painful times, but in revisiting them, I saw how far I'd come and felt a greater appreciation for my past.

Memories of my childhood best friend, Mr. Rogers, always came to mind. Throughout my childhood and across many states, he was a constant source of reassurance. While I made new friends in many places, I also had to say goodbye to them too soon, before moving on to a new location. Mr. Rogers was always there for me.

All the moving, which I loved, and the short amount of time I stayed in one place, created an inability to get past the surface with people. Without the typical, longtime childhood friends you naturally get to know over time, I would make friends and lose touch after moving away. I had friends from many places and for varying amounts of time, but each only knew the part of me from the period we shared. I couldn't bring a new friend up to speed on my life in these short amounts of time, and then I often wondered if it mattered because I never knew who would remain a friend.

But Mr. Rogers remained, and with his soft-spoken words, I knew he understood me, which brought me great comfort. His uplifting messages reminded me that I was special and loved just the way I was—what a beautiful thought.

Every time I got behind the wheel of a car, boarded a plane, or took a seat on a train or a bus, I wasn't just traveling from one place to another; I was collecting pieces and memories of the girl I was, and in doing so, furthering my mission to leave a little love behind.

One of the stops on my journey home was Nebraska. Beginning in Texas, stopping in Oklahoma, and arriving in Nebraska, I replayed many memories tucked away for safe-keeping. With each turn in the road, many experiences came flooding back to me. I had invited all three of my children to accompany me on my road trip. I wanted to show them where mommy lived, grew up, and went to school. But Jack already had plans to attend sleep-away camp for the first time, and Destiny decided to stay behind at a friend's house in Texas, where I started on this particular journey.

My hope for Lainey, who wanted to join me on this adventure, was to give her a gift I hoped she would carry with her the way I have. I hoped that this journey would change her the way it molded me. I hoped she would feel the exhilaration of adventure, and in the hours of travel, rather than feel boredom, that she would look up from the window and feel the magnitude of this world. I wanted Lainey to have the opportunities that exist if only she's brave enough to embrace them. I know she is. I hoped that Lainey would understand that circumstances are only temporary and that she has the power to overcome the challenging ones.

I hoped Lainey would discover that unresolved problems will follow you no matter where you go and that happiness is a state of mind, not a destination. I wanted her to spread her wings and discover that sometimes you just fly higher and feel more comfortable in some places more than others. I hoped Lainey would find that the journey is often more memorable than the destination itself.

To see my daughter's eyes light up with the same wonder I had, told me that she felt it, and I hoped the magic would never leave her. If Lainey is like me, she will learn to transport herself to the wide-open spaces when she needs to. She will always carry a piece of the Midwest with her, and people Lainey met who told her about me when I was close to her age will always live within her heart. My daughter left Nebraska, changed, just like I did all those years ago, and I couldn't be happier. Although my other two children didn't get to experience that road trip, they hear mommy talking about these magical moments often as I try hard to give them a glimpse of what she witnessed.

A place once filled with challenges, heartbreak, loneliness, and uncertainty was also a place that showed me great love, joy, and serenity. One little Nebraska town strengthened my faith when I was a little girl, while another filled me with experiences that tested me when I was older.

Both reminded me that good people exist and that adversity is life's equal opportunity to make or break us. Life was not easy or fair, especially in this part of the country. Hard work was a way of life, and nothing was handed to me (or anyone else) unless it was earned or blessed by God. It was the wide-open spaces that expanded my heart and my mind as vast as the great plains and uninterrupted, beautiful skies.

It was a place where the perpetual motion of tumbleweeds and freight trains reminded me of my life and the constant unpredictability of the journey. With the "smell of money," an earthy scent of manure, fresh-cut hay, and rolling thunderstorms, my little Nebraska town was the place where farmers, ranchers, railroaders, Native Americans, and those who couldn't imagine living anywhere else called home. If you claimed that one day you would "escape" that little town, like me, you know that it never leaves you, thank God.

The people who make up that area know struggle, hardship, and defeat, but they remain unchanged in conviction, with their resolve uncompromised, as their faces continue to point to the skies. Looking up, it's not what you see but what you feel that changes who you are.

It's the place where I appreciated the little things even more than before and never took for granted how hard someone had to work to produce a successful crop. Winters were harsh, and the summers were out of this world. Stars filled the sky with more sparkling lights than the dark contrast of the vast universe, and sudden storms quickly stirred up, changing beauty. More than just beef and corn, Nebraska is where many other nationally dependent vegetables are grown. Home of the original cabbage burger, and the one and only Bismark, Nebraska was deliciously unforgettable.

While I was back, I had a tire mishap, and everything in the town was closed. Every person I encountered either offered to help, provided a suggestion, or took it upon themselves to pick up the phone and call a friend. People in Nebraska don't ask if you need help; they just stretch out their hands.

If you find yourself on the side of a road, someone is bound to stop and ask if you're okay. With a flip of the hand off the steering wheel, drivers exchange waves as they pass each other on the road. It doesn't matter if you know them or not, you're all sharing this fantastic space with one another, and all encounters should be friendly and warm ones. It's not about what you have but what you do with it that matters most. Everyone spends time outdoors, sits, and converses.

There's barbecue, cornhole, sun tea, and lawn chairs for everyone. The people are proud, hardworking, kind, and respectful citizens who love their country, neighbors, and their Cornhuskers. They don't take things or people for granted. When you meet someone from Nebraska, you're bound to get a hug, and it's one you know you'll never forget. To many, the wide-open plains and the long stretches of empty roads are nothing more than vast space, but this blank canvas allowed me to choose what I wanted to see and believe.

With unobstructed, unfiltered views, this was God's canvas, and here, he made masterpieces. The once uncomfortable silence of this place became a peaceful quietness that forced me to be still, listen, reflect, and take in everything around me. I am more in-tuned with myself and others and aware of beauty because I learned to look at things with intention and appreciation. This was a small town with immense love, and looking back, I can thank my father for introducing me to this world that is now a permanent part of me.

Nebraska – small towns and big hearts.

The little church with its people who saved me. / A token of my love left behind

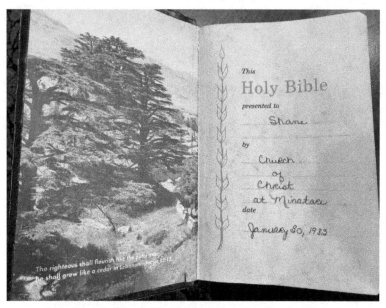

This
Holy Bible
presented to
Shane

by
Church
of
Christ
at Minatare
date
January 30, 1983

The righteous shall flourish like the palm tree.
he shall grow like a cedar in Lebanon. Psalm 92:12

My first bible, given to me by this little church

Another journey took me back to Memie and Boppie's, where I found myself in an empty lot where their house once sat. The view of the lake stirred up memories of when I was little. The trails I once walked daily are now overgrown and nearly invisible. Standing there with visions of stray cats, warm blankets, cups of tea, and Scrabble games filled my mind. I could almost taste the saltwater taffy and ribbon candy, feel the crunch of Memie's favorite toasted Lender's bagels, and smell the ocean with each helping of dulse. I thought about all the crocheted dolls, kitchen towels, and toilet paper covers she made. I smelled her Ponds cream and the many Avon fragrances she used and bought for family members. The wood-burning stove gave off comforting warmth while Willie Nelson or the weekly service at the Crystal Cathedral played on the radio.

Memie & Boppie's house once stood where all the people and animals would gather.

Atop Memie & Boppie's hill

Where I would go to take the rowboat out.
Some of the roads are now paved.

With a couple of black crow sightings, a few familiar scents, and a song on the radio that reminded me that Memie was near, I smiled as I thought about how she always spoke honestly and without hesitation, or feared what anyone thought. I remembered the great passion Memie possessed and the conviction she had for the things that mattered most to her.

As I walked down the dirt road, I remembered how strong and independent my grandmother was and how she could do everything herself. Of course, if someone extended a hand or a kind gesture, Memie never forgot. Beneath all her strength was a sensitive woman who cared for everyone and wanted to do what was right. Memie always gave people the benefit of the doubt and was serious about helping others. She was the most neighborly of neighbors. My grandmother was loyal and could be counted on when others couldn't be, but if you abused that loyalty or took her for a sucker, she never forgot that either.

Going back brought to mind Memie's passing and the closeness we shared. As I stood in the grass looking around at the familiar spots in their yard where I made cherished memories, I thought about the many conversations Memie and I shared at her kitchen table as we looked out at the water. She always confided in me and treated me as an adult because my grandmother knew I understood things. As I got older, Memie shared details with me about what she wanted at her funeral. She didn't want anything elaborate; she simply wanted me to play Barbara Streisand's *Somewhere*.

Memie knew I would execute her wish, and I did. She also said she didn't want anyone to have to pay for her funeral. Our grandmother didn't want to burden any of her children with this expense and decided to be cremated. Memie used to mention to me all the time that she wanted to donate her body to science when she died. She would say, "If it could help my family or someone else, why not?"

The idea of college students using her body as a science lesson disturbed me, so I often changed the subject. I was blessed to be by Memie's side and say goodbye to her but found out after she passed that she had arranged to have her body sent off for science purposes, and with that came a free cremation. When the "science team" was finished studying Memie's body, they returned her ashes to the family. There was no report or any further intelligence provided to us, but Memie did precisely what she wanted to do, unbeknownst and unsettling to many, especially me.

I knew that her spirit took flight the moment Memie exhaled her final breath, and she was free. Her body was just a vessel. I fulfilled her request and played my grandmother's song for her at the service. Memie knew what she was doing when she asked me, and the words of the song meant even more now.

I could only hope that somehow, her final gift to this world (her body) served a greater purpose. Perhaps it helped a young student who was studying to be a physician to learn and, in turn, heal others. Memie believed in Heaven, but she also thought that your spirit lives on in other ways and could even be reborn. I would recognize her when she came back. "I'll be a big oak tree or a beautiful crow sitting in one," she always said.

As I walked around this familiar place where there once lived so much love, I knew that she was with me and continues to be. Several years later, while in California, I visited the Crystal Cathedral that she loved to listen to weekly and knew she was with me.

The Crystal Cathedral, Garden Grove, CA

Going back to that house, where my mom sat me down in the front room and told me about her illness, brought back many memories. As I drove down a narrow dirt road that still isn't paved, I remembered playing with the neighbor kids, riding bikes, and forming a tribe of sorts. Back then, kids weren't often involved in sports or taken to various clubs and activities.

We simply came home from school, did our homework, and agreed to meet outside as quickly as possible. We spent hours upon hours outside digging in the mud and running through the cul-de-sac if you could call it that. The house looked even smaller than I remembered. I don't know if it was always as run-down looking as it is today or if I chose to look past that when I was younger and simply appreciated having a place to live together.

*The little yellow house and another dirt
road that held so many memories*

I found that my journey home helped me find greater peace and purpose in all the painful parts, while I remembered and felt a greater appreciation for all the beautiful details. Collecting these pieces and patching them together, just like one of Memie's colorful handmade blankets, brought me warmth and comfort as I wrapped myself in the memories. The collection of different shaped and sized pieces created the one-of-a-kind gift that represented my life.

Looking at it from afar gave me a better understanding of, and appreciation for, all of the pieces: the pretty ones and the painful ones, and I saw the purposes in all of them. I had a renewed sense of gratitude for all that I had seen, experienced, and overcome in my life—each step, a stone in my foundation—every broken piece, now sewn together to make a beautiful tapestry. Every choice or change of direction was a decision that brought me to where I am today. Just like the verse in the song "The House That Built Me," *I thought if I could touch this place or feel it, this brokenness inside me might start healing. Out here, it's like I'm someone else. I thought that maybe I could find myself.*[5]

Play Track 21 (The House That Built Me – Miranda Lambert) in Broken Little Believer Playlist

Baggage Check:

Have you ever returned to a place that holds special memories? Did it look or feel different to you? Did you take anything with you that you didn't arrive with? A different perspective, perhaps?

_____

_____

_____

_____

_____

_____

_____

_____

_____

_____

_____

_____

CHAPTER 22

Try

When I was in elementary school, I attended my little brother's daycare during the summer months. It became somewhat of a camp for all ages. Like most summer programs, days consisted of games, activities, snacks, lunchtimes, and of course, recess out on the playground.

There was a boy who always followed me around. He was about my age, but he seemed younger because of his annoying and relentless antics. He would taunt me, make silly comments, and follow them with, "You can't catch me, nanahna." I had no interest in chasing him, so his efforts were fruitless. When another student suggested he liked me, I was confused by that notion because his behavior was the opposite. The invitations to play his cat and mouse game continued, but this mouse was not taking the cheese.

Then, one day, he started running full force, straight toward me. Confused and a bit startled, I turned and proceeded to run in the opposite direction. Darting between playground equipment, I raced to the safety of the school. However, just before I reached the door, he managed to cut me off, and I became trapped in a corner, unable to escape.

With his arm outstretched as though he was about to tag me and say, "You're it," he grabbed on tight to my chest, which, at that time, most likely resembled his, and twisted my right breast with such unrelenting force that I cried as I tried to loosen his grip and escape from the hold.

When I finally managed to break free, I ran straight inside the school, where a teacher stopped me and asked me what happened. I was taken to the nurse and embarrassed when she asked me to pull up my shirt to assess and document the injury. When I did, she gasped to find a beet red chest and a bluish-purple outline of five fingers twisted around my pre-pubescent breast.

Spending the afternoon in the nurse's office with ice packs on my chest was not the summer memory I had hoped for or could have imagined. To this day, I can still remember that pain and the lasting marks that boy left on me both physically and mentally. The assault elicited intense reactions from me if anyone ever backed me into a corner or challenged me in a way that made me feel threatened again.

As the years went by, I finally entered the world of puberty. I was the last girl in my grade to get her period, and I didn't need a bra, but like so many other girls who got their first bra as a rite of passage, I just wanted to fit in. While many girls and their parents will say it's hard for the girls who are first to develop and get their periods, I can tell you that it's tough for those who are last, too.

But alas, though I was officially a young lady, I couldn't help but notice that my breasts were not only different sizes, they were different shapes too. My left was a teardrop shape, and my right was very round. If I were to stand in the mirror and study my changing body, I always preferred to do so with my left shoulder leading. I felt more satisfied with this angle because it had more curves and was the side I felt proud of.

However, turning to the other side, I felt a little boyish, with fewer curves and less volume. Much like my life, experiences, and the face I showed the world, my breasts represented the contrast between them. It was odd, but it was normal for me.

Life goes on, and I don't recognize these things as much anymore. After my wedding, multiple pregnancies, and breast-feeding, I reached a point when I accepted my body for what it was and capable of. To nourish my children and experience that bond for as long as I did, was a gift. I had nothing but respect for my body after that and cherished being able to give and sustain life.

And then one day, I found a mole near my areola. I went to the dermatologist, who suggested I consider going to a plastic surgeon since it was close to my nipple. This tiny mole led me down a rabbit hole that I wish I had never visited. It almost became a secondary conversation to this particular doctor who asked me if I had ever considered implants.

Shocked and almost insulted, I said, "No." He proceeded to illustrate to me how asymmetrical my breasts were as he casually handed me several different sizes and types of implants. Holding them in my hands, I wasn't quite sure what to do with them. Was I supposed to squeeze them, juggle them, or what? He suggested I "try 'em on for size," but I declined.

He then had his nurse take a couple of photos of me with my bra on—one facing forward and two standing sideways in opposite directions. Within minutes, he presented me with a collage of magically enhanced photos showing what I looked like and how I could look. I was shocked and intrigued but primarily resistant to this sales technique and opted to go elsewhere to have my mole removed.

I couldn't help but look at the photos, though, and wondered what it would be like to have two similar shaped and sized breasts. As someone who swore I would never put anything artificial in my body to enhance it, I resisted the idea but secretly dreamed about it. Of course, once it was in my head, every swimsuit, dress, or tank top I saw would look better with an evened-out set of boobs! It seemed all of my friends either had them or wanted to get them. My husband, who, in his defense, said he loved me as I was, didn't challenge the idea, and when I caught a little grin of excitement on his face, I began to feel like researching breast implants more wouldn't hurt.

I had a list of pros and cons, and if I were ever to decide to do it, I knew what I would get. They would be saline, over the muscle (not under), and they would be natural. I was a small C on the left and a small B on the right, so I would only be interested in achieving symmetry.

I spoke to all of my friends who had them, got lots of recommendations, and even went on breast augmentation sites to gain insight from other women regarding things they wish they'd known sooner or wish they had done differently. I visited with multiple doctors and had numerous consultations, and finally, after a long time of struggling with the idea, I made the decision to get breast implants.

I chose a doctor in Manhattan who not only had one of the best reputations but also happened to be one of the more expensive. I justified the cost with having greater peace of mind knowing he was highly experienced and his clientele was classy. I felt good about my decision, but I was scared.

He was thorough and sent me for lab work and professional photos of my breasts before surgery. It was these black and white photos of my breasts that solidified my decision to move forward. I had never seen a picture of my breasts from straight on. I studied these photos and wondered if that's how my husband saw them. Had he noticed the differences the way I now saw them in these photos? I convinced myself that if I could do something to safely enhance my body, feel better about myself, and be more attractive to my husband, what could be so bad?

The surgery went well, and I recovered quickly. I began to shop for new bras and was excited to find that they fit me— both breasts! I was more confident and finally felt "even." I could now proudly wear dresses and shirts that I once had to modify to avoid embarrassment or feelings of insecurity.

All this enthusiasm was short-lived, though, as I started to have issues. My right breast started to tighten up and became distorted, leaving me in pain. My doctor informed me that I was experiencing capsulation, where the body rejects a foreign object and begins to form scar tissue around it. Scar tissue was forming quickly, and as it did, it pulled tighter and tighter on my chest.

I was ready to have them taken out and be done with it. I was scared and regretting my decision. My doctor talked me into allowing him to repair the damage, saying that it would be a "waste" not to try. After much deliberation, I agreed to let him replace that implant and hoped and prayed for the best.

Sadly, within months, the same thing happened again, and this time, I was through. Just like the mole, I had them removed and wished the doctor had never suggested the procedure.

Play Track 22 (TRY – Colbie Caillat) in Broken Little Believer Playlist

Baggage Check:

Are you using fancy, expensive luggage to compensate for insecurity or lack of confidence? Are you hiding behind the image of a "sleek" or confident traveler, or have you accepted that you are on an uncertain journey and all the wear and tear shows how far you've traveled?

_____

_____

_____

_____

_____

_____

_____

_____

_____

_____

_____

CHAPTER 23

Good Good Father

Jenn and I were neighbors, but "destiny" brought us together. I had spoken to her on the blacktop of our children's school many times, and I knew that Jenn was hiding a secret. I never brought it up out of respect and only hoped she would feel comfortable enough to open up to me one day.

A married mom of two girls, Jenn was beautiful—even with a wig and a crocheted hat hiding what had been taken from her. Her big, bright smile lit up rooms, and with a kind, genuine, and considerate heart, you instantly knew she was special. She had a contagious laugh, a sarcastic sense of humor, and a fierce and unshakeable sense of loyalty when it came to those for whom she loved and cared.

We had just taken a child into our home, and as destiny would have it, she was placed in Jenn's oldest daughter's class. There was no hiding either one of our secrets, and we shuffled off to a corner of the blacktop to share, confidentially, what we were trying to keep from others. Although she had been diagnosed with breast cancer and had beaten it once, she had experienced an aggressive recurrence.

In our private conversations, we quickly got to know one another and became fast friends. I shared that we were foster parents and that the new girl in her daughter's class had just been placed in our home. Our latest addition to the family, Destiny would bring our children and us closer together.

Jenn disclosed many things, and in turn, I opened up to her. We shared many of the same perspectives and beliefs, and as we got to know each other well, we found that we had even more in common with one another than we initially realized. Having been around family and friends who had been sick and the awareness I had of the C-word gave me a greater understanding and sensitivity to her many emotions.

Knowing the profound effect that words have on people and the power they carry, I knew what Jenn needed and wanted, and it was easy for me to be an uplifting, positive, and supportive friend. When she headed down a lonely path of fear and anxiety, I found ways to distract Jenn and redirect her thoughts. I understood her loneliness and recognized the feelings of despair she felt. Even when Jenn was surrounded by people and tried desperately to enjoy herself, voices of worry and doubt would creep in and try to rob her of her peace. She found it reassuring that I understood this and that I wasn't afraid to tell those voices to shut up, teaching Jenn to stand up to them too.

During our friendship, Jenn and I crammed in adventures, laughs, and tears. Whether it was countless laps around our neighborhood or making one of many dreaded trips into the city for her doctor appointments, we always enjoyed our time together. It felt like she and I had known each other much longer than we had. Perhaps the looming uncertainty that existed helped us be more open, honest, and genuine with each other.

SHANE SVOREC

Jenn and I accompanied each other to nutritionists, chiropractors, traditional and alternative medicine doctors, and many specialists. We visited salt caves, had Reiki sessions, attended healing masses, and spent time at holistic medicine centers. We drank protein shakes and green (gag) smoothies, clutched crystals, used essential oils, listened to Christian music, and repeated many prayers for her healing, peace, and understanding.

There wasn't much we didn't do or try to improve the quality of Jenn's life and increase the time she had to live it. We believed in healing, and if my friend ever doubted that power was possible, I was there to remind her that it was. I prayed for her all the time.

We cherished our time together and always made the most of it. In waiting rooms, on car rides, or just sitting next to each other in one another's living rooms, back yards, or front patios, we had many long, meaningful conversations and shared quite a few secrets. Even when she felt awful, she maintained her sense of humor.

As I drove her to a treatment in the city one day, the stop-and-go traffic left her feeling nauseated. She turned to me and said, "Do you mind if I put the window down?"

"Of course not," I responded, "Go right ahead." As she put her entire head out the window, she positioned her face forward in the direction we were going. Little wisps of hair sticking out from her hat flew in the wind as she breathed in deeply and said, "Ahhhhh.....the smell of urine in New York City!" We couldn't stop laughing. As she took in the "not so fresh air," what she dished out was priceless.

There wasn't a day that went by that Jenn and I didn't talk, text, or see each other. We became inseparable, and when my friend had to go to the hospital unexpectedly, her girls would come and stay at our house.

I watched Jenn endure more than any person should have to. I hated to watch it all, and when she waited on test results and phone calls, I waited with her. All I could do was encourage and support Jenn and reassure my friend that she would never be alone. She jokingly referred to me as "mommy" because I always had my hand on her or held onto her when we walked. My dear friend came to know that when I said, "I have you, and I'll never let go," I meant it.

Many nights I would lie awake in bed crying as I thought about all Jenn had been through and the suffering she continued to experience. Still, this angel maintained a smile on her face or had quick-witted remarks that would shock and entertain those around her.

She suffered multiple setbacks, including a fall, a broken bone, and a few seizures, but even in her weakened state, she was determined to walk up my front steps to hug me and bring me flowers when I unexpectedly lost my cousin Mark. There wasn't anything she wouldn't do for someone she loved, and she knew how much my cousin meant to me.

Mark and I were friends growing up, but after his mom passed, we became even closer. His mom was my mother's bone marrow match, and my aunt saved her life as her donor all those years ago. Mark had a heart of gold, loved everyone, and never forgot anything, although he was disabled. We often reminisced about our younger years, times spent at Memie and Boppie's, and all the fun we had. We would talk on the phone regularly, and I made many visits to see him. Mark's sudden passing left me with a sense of deep sadness, and the only peace and comfort I found were in knowing that he was reunited with his mom.

A few months earlier, we had taken in an eighteen-year-old high school senior who was down on her luck and didn't have a place to stay. She was only going to be with us for a few months, so I was busy trying to help her get a job, her driver's license, and set up with a checking and savings account before she went out into the world on her own. It was a stressful time, and some of her behaviors and rule-breaking only compounded my anxiety.

Several weeks after driving Jenn to the hospital where she was admitted, a decision was made to move her to a hospice facility. The weeks that followed were some of the most painful and heartbreaking thus far. I continued to spend every moment I could with her. I knew all the nurses, the daily and evening routines, and the quiet, beautiful, and peaceful spots I would push her in the wheelchair. We sat in the garden out by the Mother Mary statue, went inside to pray in the chapel, and went out back to feel the warm breeze and sun upon our faces.

One day I picked up the kids from school, dropped them off at home, and headed back to spend the evening with her. As I walked into her room, where she was sitting in the recliner, she immediately signaled me to come over to her. She wanted to speak to me. As I kneeled in front of her and put my hands on her knees, she placed her hands over mine and started to cry.

I asked her what was wrong and what I could do for her, but she just said she loved me—"my Louise." We always had a backup plan in place should I need to "break her (Thelma) out"—her words. I tried to keep my emotions boarded up tightly, but they burst free as she cried. I could no longer hold my tears back, and they fell with hers. It was the first time that I wasn't the strong and positive one.

I told her how much I loved her too, but what she said next left me speechless. In a soft and tired voice, she thanked me for saving her. "Saving her?" I thought. As my tears fell even harder, I was convinced the meds had caused her some confusion, but she continued and said, "Shanie, you have filled every one of my holes. You saved me."

The battened-down doors of my tightly packed heart had been ripped off, and I could no longer control the tears, let alone stop them. The beauty of Jenn's words and the love I felt in them brought a sense of peace and light to the darkness closing in. I also couldn't ignore the pain I felt, knowing that "saving her" was all I wanted but ultimately couldn't do in every way. This irony was a sharp pain caused by a beautiful blunt force.

After that day, she didn't say much, and I knew she had chosen her words and the time she decided to share them with me carefully. A few days later, I stayed the night with her. My nightly routine included turning on the diffuser with a relaxing, scented essential oil, quietly playing some of our favorite songs, cracking the door to bring in a little light, and setting the temperature just right. I had slept in the reclining chair before, but this night, I pushed it up against her bedrail so I could reach her hand. I watched her as she slept and gently rested my hand on her shoulder as I told her that I would never leave her, and I didn't.

I fought to stay awake, and when my eyes closed and my head jerked forward, I would quickly open my eyes in a panic to be sure I didn't miss a moment with her. As I looked at her, I couldn't help but be amazed by her strength. Each time they gave her something to help with the pain, she responded less. As the time drew nearer, she kept fighting. It was heartbreaking. A nurse told me that it wasn't going to be easy because she was a young mother with many reasons to live. I understood this and thought of my mom's near-death experience and the hesitation she felt going to the light because she didn't want to leave us. Of course, this nurse was right, but Jenn was also stronger than any other woman I knew. It would be at her time and on her terms.

Even when she wasn't able to talk, I knew she was there, aware, and I hated that she had struggled with letting go. That night, as I watched her and kept my hand on her shoulder, I played a song she loved—*Good Good Father*. I nodded off momentarily for the last time when I awoke to a hand on my shoulder. I jumped up in shock, initially thinking it was

Jenn reaching back out to me, but when I looked up from the recliner, I saw the night nurse who whispered, "She's gone."

"How?" I asked. "I was just looking at her and saw her breathing."

She gently said, "It's ok. She just passed."

I knew she wouldn't go while I was watching her, but no matter how many times I told her that I loved her, would always watch over her girls, or never forget her, I felt like I could have said it one more time.

I knew she was at peace. In my semi-alert state, I had a vision of her standing on top of a mountain. Before Jenn was a beautiful, bright, warm, and welcoming light leading to paradise, and behind her, all the people she knew and loved. I felt like the nurse's hand on my shoulder was Jenn's hand and that she did say goodbye to me because, in my vision, she smiled at me and at all those who loved her and waved goodbye. As she walked into Heaven, the song she loved was playing.

Jenn died on May 25, 2018, one month after I lost my cousin, Mark. I tried to hold the house together and keep a smile on my face for our kids and hers. I struggled to deal with the defiant behaviors of a teen I wanted to help while saying goodbye to the most beautiful soul I have ever had the privilege of calling a friend. My life felt like it was falling apart, and the grief was too much to bear.

The year that followed her passing was one of the darkest years of my life. I felt grief, anger, confusion, heartache, speculation, distrust, and resentment. I sensed that I processed these challenging feelings differently than most. I internalized things and couldn't let them go. Even the pain was precious to me, and it was hard to release.

The entire time I was friends with Jenn, she was sick or undergoing treatment. There was never a time when we could go out, party, or even have drinks. Instead, we cherished the little things and focused on what was most important. We had no choice but to discuss life, death, and what we believed and hoped would happen afterward.

My friend and I had filled our short journeys and adventures with many memories that would last forever. It was one of the most painful experiences I've ever known—to watch someone I loved go through so much, and as a mother, to see the pain and worry Jenn had for her children. It left me with a grief I found nearly impossible to let go.

But despite the pain, I wouldn't have traded a single moment I had being by Jenn's side because every second I spent with her was precious and filled with love, care, and honesty. She touched my life in such a profound way that I will never be the same, and while I didn't have the gift of knowing her the longest, I knew Jenn in her bleakest time, and I could not be any prouder of the woman she was, the example she set, and the legacy she left behind.

There was nothing more important to me, no more incredible privilege or honor than to be by Jenn's side and offer comfort, peace, love, and friendship. I was blessed to have been able to fill her holes, but I now had a giant, gaping one in my heart, and I didn't have her to help fill it or patch mine.

I would have to go on being strong for Jenn's girls and others. I would take the emotional outbursts, insecurities, and assumptions of some and turn the other cheek. I would hold it all in because Jenn knew I could and would. Jenn made me promise her many things, and giving her my word was an honor and something that didn't require convincing. No matter how much my heart might hurt, she told me to "always keep it open" and to continue to inspire others.

"Write your book," Jenn often told me. This prospect felt like nearly unbearable pain, though, and I questioned it. I knew she was in a better place and was finally free of suffering, but I felt it was unfair for those of us left behind who loved and missed her, especially her girls. She told me she would send me lots of signs to let me know that she was with me, and Jenn didn't waste any time doing so.

Life is very different now. Her family, whom she loved beyond measure, will always bring memories of her strength and determination to my mind. The unrelenting will she possessed and the courage she demonstrated as she fought long and hard for her husband and children continue to be felt as her spirit remains with them.

Play Track 23 (Good Good Father – Chris Tomlin) in Broken Little Believer Playlist

Baggage Check:

Have you ever felt like throwing it all away—your luggage, that is? Have you ever experienced how insignificant all you carry is when a road comes to an abrupt end? Have you stopped and considered that much of the baggage you take and the luggage you pack may not be essential and may even be weighing you down?

_____

_____

_____

_____

_____

_____

_____

_____

_____

_____

CHAPTER 24

Run to the Father

A year of "firsts" had passed, and we were celebrating Jenn's life and her husband's birthday, both on May 25th, with a get-together of close friends and family in their backyard. I had just gone for a mammogram a few days earlier and was awaiting additional information. I've always had cystic breasts, so going for follow-up images or ultrasounds was nothing new for me.

I was always diligent with my wellness visits, and having no family history of breast cancer, I should have been at ease, but this time was different. To make matters worse, and adding to my emotional hurricane, the timing of this anticipated news happened within days of my dear friend's passing just one year earlier. It felt like cruel and unusual punishment.

With a boot on my right foot and a gimp in my step, the result of tripping over one of our dogs and breaking my big toe in several places, I made my way up the elevator and down the hall. I checked in and waited and then waited some more. At one point, the nurse who periodically appeared from behind a door to call patients back looked at me and then down at my boot with a bit of confusion and stated, "I believe you want the second floor. Orthopedics is downstairs."

"No, I've already had my bottom half looked at, thank you. I'm here for my top half today." After that clarification, it was the usual routine: "Take this gown and get undressed from the waist up, with the opening in the front. You can leave your things in here and take a seat in the waiting room just outside."

It's always a bit awkward sitting with unfamiliar women donning robes, knowing we are all bare-chested underneath. I'm the person who always tries to make small talk and create a community out of a mixed group. I can't help but observe the mood of those in the room. Across age, ethnicity, size, and shape, we are all here for the same reason, and none of us are excited to be poked, prodded, and squeezed.

Some come with books, while others are busy scrolling through their phones, and almost everyone keeps their head down. I'm not too fond of this situation and decide to smile and say hello as I find a seat. Some women complain about having to wait and proceed to mention all the things they have to do, while others gripe about the room temperature, the parking, or some other thing. I hear discontent about insurance, which procedures are covered, and which ones aren't.

But whether someone is complaining or reading, each one seems to want to distract herself from overthinking. Like everyone else, I anxiously sit in the chair as, one by one, we are called in. Everyone worries about a callback for a second image.

I was more nervous this time. My breasts were always different, and my right one was always problematic. I had felt more of a difference in this breast recently, which was eerily reminiscent of when I had experienced capsulation of my implant. It was hard, full, and painful. I thought perhaps the empty cavity where the implant once was had filled with fluid again and hoped it just needed draining. It didn't make me any less anxious or worried, but it wasn't an unfamiliar or new problem for me. I had been down this road before, unfortunately.

As most women do, I cringed and held my breath as the machine began to clamp down, and the vice tightened against my right breast. For the first time since I started getting mammograms, I shed a couple of silent tears as I held my breath when instructed, then winced as I let out a heavy breath and, "Oh my God!" when the nurse permitted me to "breathe" again. "It hurts!" I said forcefully. The technician apologized but continued. Once the image was captured and the machine let go of its painful grip, she came over to reposition my breast and said, "Have you experienced any discharge from your breasts?"

I emphatically replied, "No, never!" As the technician wiped the surface of the breast-holding plate, she said, "Well, you had some just now." With a rapidly beating heart and short, shallow breaths, my fear tried to debunk her observation, and I suggested it might have been from the previous person.

I didn't even consider how absurd that must have sounded, but I was scrambling to come up with some sort of explanation to make this less scary. The last time fluid came out of my breasts was when my babies nursed, and that's how I wanted to remember it.

Sensing my fear, she assured me that it wasn't much and that it "sometimes happens upon compression," but now I was even more afraid. I told myself it must mean my feelings were accurate, and I had likely just built up fluid again. The technician sent me back to the "holding room," where I saw some of the same women, along with a few new ones. I didn't feel like smiling this time, but I did. I still didn't feel like hearing the complaining either, but I listened.

I was called back for an ultrasound to get a better view. That turned into not one but three painful fine needle aspirations.

"Deep breath, Shane. One, two, three . . . little pinch." Except it wasn't a "little" pinch. It hurt . . . A LOT—all three of them.

Again, the technician sent me back out to the holding room with a few ice packs, and this time, the continuous complainer was sharing that she had to have an area biopsied. I finally said, "I just had three." It was amazing how quickly her complaints turned into sympathy and kindness, but I didn't want that either. I was still optimistic and prayerful and had hoped, like several times before, that the results would be clear and the fluid would just need to be aspirated. If this was the case, I hoped that it would also lessen the discomfort and fullness I currently experienced.

Hours and many tests later, they told me they would need to get additional tests and perform more in-depth biopsies. The day morphed into a blur. I left, not with the worst news, but for the first time, not knowing. There were still more tests ahead, including a breast MRI and several deep tissue biopsies. I was devastated, scared, and alone. My husband tried to reassure me that everything would be okay and it was probably nothing, but I couldn't help the words that left my lips. "You don't normally have three biopsies after going in for a routine mammogram and then get additional biopsies and an MRI for nothing."

The next day, I got a call from the hospital. The woman on the line was following up to schedule the additional tests and determine which should come first. She informed me that two of the pathology reports were inconclusive, so they needed more tissue. One sample showed cells they wanted to see more of. My heart dropped. I was home alone and paced the floors as I listened and asked more questions. She didn't sugarcoat anything and told me what she thought it was. I couldn't catch my breath.

My husband just happened to stop by the house to pick something up at the time and saw me pacing and crying. The woman, now asking me if I was home alone, wanted to get me in that day if possible. I could sense her urgency and concern as I struggled to process all the overwhelming and terrifying information I'd heard in a short amount of time. She asked me if I could come in that afternoon, and they would squeeze me in for some deep tissue biopsies. "Of course," I replied. My day was now shot, so, yes, I would be there.

On May 29, 2019, I wore out the floor in our house as I paced in a methodical circular pattern, repeatedly saying to myself, *I'm not special. I'm not immune.* The only thing I said more than this was, *I don't understand,* and I said it over and over and over again.

I expect that I won't ever understand, and I accept that sometimes it's just not my place, but I can honestly say that this was one of the scariest days of my life. This was the day when the one who inspired and encouraged others, the one known as "The Look Up Girl" was pushed to the brink, forced to look over the edge, and face one of her worst fears alone.

It was the day that no one could say anything to comfort me or assure me that all would be okay. It was just me, trapped among my thoughts, fears, and questions to which there were no escaping. I spent the day pacing the floors, crying out loud, thinking of my kids and husband, and facing the ugly "what if's" that seeped into my mind without permission and haunted me with every breath.

The one question I knew not to ask was "why." I knew better. It was not a question I would, or wanted, to have answered. I wouldn't dare ask, *why me?* I had learned how this worked. Cancer has no prejudices, no age limits, or discriminations of heart. *Why not me?* This question was easier to comprehend.

So, instead, over and over again, I just kept saying, *I don't understand.* I'm certainly not the first, nor would I be the last to have a day like today. Still, it was the day when the "strong one" had to figure out how to apply all the hard-learned lessons I had endured, put my gift of positivity, courage, and faith to use, spring into action, and test my limits.

As I waited and tried not to worry, thoughts and questions filled my head. Had I done this to myself? Had I created the issue that now existed? Was the pain I now felt self-inflicted or the result of wounds my heart had sustained?

As I sat in a silent room with my noisy thoughts, I remembered the painful truth and lonely reality that people don't often say what we want or need them to say, and it's not that they don't care. It's just that they don't feel things the way we do and cannot provide what our heart needs. *You come into this world alone, and you leave it alone.* Memie's words were ringing in my ear, and at that moment, I realized what she meant. On some roads, we have to travel alone. It's what I've done a lot, but I always wished I didn't have to.

My husband drove me to my appointment as I sat silently in the passenger seat, looking out the window as if watching a movie. Upon checking me in, the man at the registration desk cheerfully said, "Hey, didn't I just see you yesterday?" Mustering up a response, I simply said, "Yep, you did." I could see in his eyes that he wanted to take back his question, or at least the way he asked, because we both knew that if I was back, it likely wasn't for a good reason. "Well, at least it's Friday," he said. *Yeah, at least it's Friday,* I thought.

He told us to take a seat in the waiting room and that I would be called back shortly. I could not believe this was happening to me. It was one year since Jenn left us, and all I could hear her saying to me over and over again was, "This will never happen to you." She said it all the time, and it always made me uncomfortable. Never say never. I prayed it wouldn't, but I knew cancer didn't play fair. Jenn would follow that regular comment up with something else, but it never made me feel better.

When the nurse called me back, my husband stood up and asked if he could go with me. She told him he could but asked him to wait a few minutes while I was put in a room and changed, and then she would come back out and get him. Once again, she instructed me to remove the upper half of my clothes, gown opening in the front. I didn't hear the rest of the instructions. I wasn't sure if I was supposed to wait there and she would come back for me or if I was supposed to go to the waiting room.

I was in a different changing area, and the hallway was not familiar to me, so I didn't know where the waiting room was from there. I stepped out and stood there a bit. I looked up and down the hallway to see if I could spot the nurse who brought me to the changing area, but there was no one in sight. Holding my belongings, I peeked around the corner one last time before deciding to stay and wait.

As I stood there, it felt like I was in a bad dream. I wanted to pinch myself and awake from it. I read every sign, saw every notice, and studied every arrow pointing to the hospital's departments and wings. They scared me and left me feeling lost. There wasn't a single arrow I wanted to follow. The only one I wanted to see was the one I didn't see—home. As I stood waiting at the corner of one hallway, I fell apart.

The tears fell faster than I could wipe them away with my hands, and my robe had run out of dry places to wipe them. Just then, a nurse who appeared to be heading to her break approached me and asked if I needed help. It seemed an odd question because I had only been told what to do, where to go, and what to expect for the past few days. No one had asked me if they could help me.

I completely fell apart then, and just as quickly as she had appeared, the nurse disappeared momentarily to hurry around the corner for a box of tissues that she gently offered me. Standing there with her lunch bag in hand, she asked me what was wrong, what she could do for me, and if there was someone she could get for me. This nurse who was heading to her break, with no obligation to me as a patient, went out of her way to ask me what no one else had, and ironically, I couldn't answer.

I fumbled over my words between the tears I couldn't keep up with, and she offered me a hug. I finally managed to explain that I was waiting for a room and my husband. Before I could finish my sentence, the original nurse returned and rudely dismissed her, saying, "I've got this."

I will never forget that woman's kindness or the effort she made while on her break. On her way to rest, she chose to stop and help me, and she made a difference. She made that day a little more bearable.

My memory of everything is crystal clear from that fuzzy day. I could tell you what the ceiling looked like, how many light bulbs there were, and what number was handwritten up near the center light—4/17.

"I guess that's when they changed the light bulbs last. Four-seventeen." I said. Confused and wondering what I was talking about, everyone in the room looked at me funny until I pointed up at the date on the ceiling. I had studied and focused on that area for over an hour. I still paid attention to little details that others overlooked, but now I didn't want to see them.

I noticed the harsh sounds, forceful pressure, cold table, and instruments, the conversations that didn't include me but were held in my presence and were about me. The moments of kindness and the empty ones. The glimmer of hope, followed by the crashing weight and suffocating helplessness. The questions, exhaustion, and information overload until I finally heard, "That's enough for today. It's a lot to take in in a short amount of time. You were brave, and you did well."

The personnel all agreed, but I didn't feel brave. I did what I had to do. I didn't choose this path, and I wasn't traveling this road by choice, but it became painfully clear that it was now part of my journey, and one I found I had to travel much of alone. There was no avoiding my illness or getting off this road. I must step on the gas and keep moving forward. I didn't like where I was headed, but I could only hope it would bring me to a better place, with a brighter outcome and a favorable resolution.

Holding Mary's hand didn't feel natural at first, but she was kind and wanted to help. To distract me, she suggested we start by counting backward from 100. I initially thought it was silly! How could counting possibly distract me from what was happening? But we did this two or three more times until the doctor said, "Maybe you should start counting down from 1,000." I didn't need to count anymore. I was over it, just like I wanted what was happening to be over.

As I rested my right arm above my head and placed the back of my hand on my forehead, she asked me what the tattoo on my wrist represented. "It's a feather," I said. "It means a lot to me." I recited the saying, "When feathers appear, angels are near," and followed it by announcing, "I have many." I also shared the Bible verse that tied into the meaning of my tattoo. "He will cover you in His feathers, and under His wings, you will find refuge." Psalm 91:4

She asked if I'd repeat it, but this time for me. It took me a second to understand what she meant, but I cried as I said the words. My nurse couldn't help but notice that my feather was positioned directly over me as my hand rested on my forehead. "It's true," she said, "the Bible verse," as she pointed to my feather tattoo and where it lay. Kindness filled some moments, but emptiness still filled them more.

The thing is, I knew. I knew something was wrong. I could feel it. Despite my fear, though, I scheduled my mammogram and dragged myself to the appointment. I only prayed that Jenn's words were true and it would never happen to me. I felt guilty, wishing she was right, but sick to my stomach, she had to experience it.

I hated what it did to her, what it stole from her, what it caused. It wasn't immediate, but she would follow up her comment, "it will never happen to you" with, "but if it does, I only hope you have a friend that is as good to you as you are to me." These conversations brought tears to my eyes and still do.

Sometimes it felt like a big joke, a trick, or a bad dream. How could this be happening, and almost exactly one year after losing Jenn? I replayed every moment in my head, and the memory was torture. Being close to her and seeing all she went through—the pain, fear, sounds, smells, anxiousness, and dread, was all too much. I recounted the nights I drove home crying from the hospice center and then weeping more once I got home.

I wanted to take the pain away from her, soothe, comfort, and do anything to make it better. Now, after a year of "firsts" behind us, I found myself sitting in this dark place of dread questioning her predictions of never. What a cruel joke to find myself in this position and not have my friend by my side. As I waited on more test results to come back, all I could say was, "I don't understand. I JUST DON'T UNDERSTAND!"

Through the heartache, my only concern was for my kids. Somehow, I managed to deliver end-of-the-year speeches at a retirement dinner and my daughter's graduating class. I survived a family get-together for the Fourth of July and my son and eldest daughter's birthdays. I dropped off Jenn's and my daughters at camp without telling them anything.

I didn't want to ruin any of their celebrations or summer activities and just had to get through it all. I also didn't wish Jenn's daughters to feel any familiar feelings or experience any painful reminders that would torture them, so I stayed firm. It's what I do.

After some disappointing care at one hospital, I found a phenomenal breast surgeon who connected me with all her professional partners who came together to develop my care plan. If there was a "dream team" of doctors, they were it! I had made it this far without telling my kids, other family members, and friends, thinking it was best to focus on the task at hand.

I could manage my emotions and keep my attitude and perceptions in check, but I didn't have the strength to field others' questions, fears, or assumptions. A friend I thought would be there for me disappointed me, and I couldn't take any more loneliness. I decided not to have any expectations and to carry the pain myself. I divulged my diagnosis to three friends, who, just like the tape, were my three Ms. Each was a separate friend from a different season in my life; the reason for our connection was God's plan, and I couldn't have been more grateful.

I underwent a double mastectomy, had twelve weeks of chemo, twenty-five rounds of radiation, and a year's worth of treatment every three weeks. I lost every hair on my body, except the hair on my head, because I used the "Cold Cap Scalp Cooling System" to preserve it. Looking back, I don't know how I continued working and managing everyday life without telling people what I was going through.

In doing so, I saw life from a brand-new perspective. It was crystal clear and unfiltered, to be without any special treatment. I watched as people behaved poorly and used silly excuses like running late as a reason to be mean, rude, or inconsiderate of others. I watched as people fought with each other over things that mean nothing in the grand scheme of things.

I thought back on my days of singing on street corners with my youth group and how important it was to reach people and minister in times of loneliness or uncertainty. I realized that part of my purpose was to use my pain, not as an excuse, but as a platform to reach others.

As "The Look Up Girl," I began to minister and share messages that I wished someone had shared with me. In doing so, many reached out and told me how much they needed to hear what I wrote and shared. I knew my pain was not in vain, and I only prayed that my purpose would ensure many, many more years here with my family.

Play Track 24 (Run to The Father – Cody Carnes) in Broken Little Believer Playlist

Baggage Check:

Would you trade your baggage with someone else? Have you ever thought that someone else has more than you or travels an easier journey, only to find out that their life is not as it appears? Do you practice a life of gratitude?

_____

_____

_____

_____

_____

_____

_____

_____

_____

_____

CHAPTER 25

Anyway

During difficult times or tragedies, the people by your side may surprise you. There are those you expect to be there for you but might not be, and others you wouldn't think might show concern but do. Life has a way of opening our eyes, and mine opened to truths that have brought me painful clarify and uncomfortable solidity. There will be people who care, and those who don't, and some who want to help but don't know how. The point is, it really doesn't matter who isn't there or their reasons why, but who IS there is what matters most.

When my husband and I said our wedding vows, I believed he would fulfill his end of the bargain, but "for better or for worse, in sickness and in health?" Just the thought of putting those vows to the test made me cringe, fearful that I might be disappointed. I could have never imagined the depths of his love or the extent of his devotion had I not walked down that dark and lonely path of a cancer diagnosis. I felt blessed to have his love and see our vows in action.

While I would never, **ever** wish to experience anything like that again or have to go through cancer, it was in that hell that I saw the purest, most beautiful, and potent love, affection, support, and devotion. He proved himself a million times over, and I was brought to tears by his care and tenderness while my heart filled with gratitude.

To be by my side was one thing, but to change dressings, drain tubes, apply bandages and administer medications was new to him. At the same time, he kept the house running and paid bills, all while telling me I was beautiful despite my loss of femininity, emotional distress, and incapacity. It was an unexpected gift in a dark storm.

Knowing my husband and my "adopted Dad" both loved me meant everything right and nothing wrong. Tom called me one night as I sat in a school parking lot waiting to lead a Board of Education meeting. He matter-of-factly told me he had been diagnosed with pancreatic cancer.

Tom and Barbara had just landed in Florida, where they traditionally spent their winters. They stopped at a hospital on the way to their condo so he could have some problematic symptoms checked and received the diagnosis. I held my breath and remained strong for him. We shared positive, determined, quiet strength and chose to focus only on what we could control.

He optimistically shared the details about chemo and, with a chuckle, announced that he wouldn't lose his hair. I bit my tongue. I was currently living the treatment routine he described, but I intended to keep my diagnosis to myself until I completed everything. I was determined to save him the worry about anything but himself and his health.

Less than two months later, I said goodbye to the man who had been an inspiration to me, of unrelenting dedication and unwavering support throughout my life. I had just completed radiation and was still undergoing treatment, unbeknownst to everyone. I walked into Tom's hospital room and stumbled into every emotion I didn't want to feel. The painful memories I fought so hard to forget during Jenn's hospice stay came flooding back.

I couldn't possibly say goodbye to Tom. Not now, not this way! This separation wasn't supposed to happen. Only a few months earlier, I had been a surprise guest speaker at his induction into the New York State Middle School Hall of Fame. It was such a beautiful evening and a well-deserved celebration. To have the opportunity to speak about the mark he made in education and the impact he had on my life was an honor and privilege. The following is an excerpt from my speech:

> After middle school, Tom Kane and I remained in touch. Across many miles and states, through many life events, including high school and college graduation, career changes, personal celebrations, and various monumental milestones, we remained connected. Every letter and email, signed in a way that has become a long-standing tradition, is now a timeless reminder of a very special connection that, although I did not initially expect, I have long appreciated and will forever cherish.
>
> My early impressions of him in the hallways of Nyack Middle School have since become a larger collection of memories that I am grateful to have been able to add to over these many years.
>
> Tom Kane made a mark so positive and powerful that he was asked to walk a former student down the aisle on one of her most important days. . . her wedding day. Today, seventeen years later, it is now my honor to be here to celebrate **his** joyous occasion and to witness him accept his well-deserved honor of being inducted into the Middle School Hall of Fame.
> Congratulations and "*TSC of YSS and LYL*!"

I could never have imagined I would be delivering his eulogy just a few short months later. With my burnt skin peeling beneath my clothes from radiation and my thoughts and emotions racing out of control, I told him how much I loved him, how much he meant to me, and the gift he was to me in my life.

Acknowledging and agreeing to follow through on his many loving, fatherly instructions, I repeated all the things he always made me promise: to do something for me for a change, to finish writing my book, to slow down and relax a bit, and always to take special care of my special self.

Tom was not my father, but he chose to be my dad, and I will forever be grateful. His wife, Barbara, is another gift he gave me, and I am thankful for our relationship and her presence in my life and that of my family. I never told him what I was hiding, but I knew that once he made his way to Heaven, he would become a mighty angel among my beautiful and powerful army of angels in the sky.

I completed my treatments and rang the bell. I've undergone multiple reconstructive phases and have begun anew. I am not the same woman I was before, but I am the woman I am today and will be tomorrow because of God's grace, love, and mercy.

"

You robbed me of my peace
Now I demand it back
You don't own me, define me, or hold me down
I despise you, refute you
Your existence, I condemn
I'm the girl you shouldn't have messed with
I'm the woman whose fury you unleashed within
Your name has no power over me
My will you have tested
I abolish your presence
In my faith, I have rested
I've been kind and patient while resisting your sorrow
You tried hard to beat me, and my life you selfishly borrowed
But the time has come, when I take it back
I will stare you down until you back away
I will not cower in defense
Instead I will face you and stand in my truth
My life is not yours, it's His to use

SHANE SVOREC

The Look Up Girl
POSITIVE LIVING

Unanswered cries and desperation taught me to rely on my faith, focus on the possible, and seek the truth. Throughout my life, I have developed a strength that many have underestimated and misunderstood. This inner strength I've mustered has helped me survive, but it has also harmed me. The perception that others have of me has often resulted in one of two scenarios. People either assumed I didn't need or want help or didn't know how or if they should help me.

This balancing act of needing and wanting was a challenge to manage. I couldn't let my guard down but had to be capable of surviving. When those closest to me were absent, I realized this conflicting phenomenon was just as confusing to others as it was to me. I felt like I was one of the most transparent people around. But when a long-time friend casually said to me one day, "You know, I kind of hate how strong you are, Shane," I realized that my necessary pursuit of resilience often gave others the impression that I wanted to go it alone or do things on my own.

The truth was, I hated how invincible I was sometimes and resented that I even had to be. I didn't ask to be tough. I made it a point to never pray for strength for fear that God might give me more to carry, because as the saying goes, "God only gives us what we can handle."

Instead, I made it a habit to pray for understanding, guidance, peace, and comfort. I prayed that I might be a better wife, mother, daughter, sister, neighbor, and friend. Then, as I got older, my prayers matured along with my faith. While I still prayed for all those same things, I began to pray that I would have the wisdom to recognize my purpose, the passion to fulfill it, and the courage to accept it.

I thought life would get easier as I got older. I felt like I had checked off many "firsts" before my time: my first job, my first apartment, my first set of bills, my first car payment, etc. I had hoped that all my young, premature experience would have given me an advantage (or maybe just a little breathing room while others my age were busy checking off the firsts that I already had under my belt).

But life has a way of unfolding at different speeds and in various forms for all people. Like it or not, I realized that I was being prepared for more, and my coping and survival skills would continue to expand. There was no resting as life unfolded.

When I look back, I feel like I've lived several lifetimes—each version of me leading one step closer to where and who I am today. I continue to believe and take comfort in the thought that the things I've experienced have not only helped to prepare me for more considerable challenges, but they might also serve to help someone else.

My faith has become stronger through it all, and my heart has become more loving (even when it aches). I am grateful for my husband and my children, and I am blessed to have patient and understanding friends. I have found they express love and care in many ways, and I am grateful for the ways they've shown me concern and devotion. I don't always know what lesson each part of my journey will serve to provide, but I always know that it will be one in His name and for His glory.

Spending so much of my life traveling and moving around the country, it's natural that I relate to and find symbolism in comparing life to a ride. We're always in motion, but at different speeds, adjusting to new terrains and finding alternative paths when detours or unexpected delays impede our travel.

How we respond to accidents, running out of gas, or breaking down and waiting, hoping, praying for help to come is vital. Do we cancel the trip because it started badly, or do we regroup, plan, and try again? Do we get upset when we encounter detours, or do we appreciate the views we would not have enjoyed otherwise?

When we get turned around and are behind schedule, do we react frantically when asking for directions or use the opportunity to chat with the person we would have never met if not for the inconvenient recalculation? Have you ever considered that the person who helped you on the side of the road just might be an angel in disguise?

I've encountered many angels throughout my life and have drawn strength and encouragement from even the simplest exchanges. The eyes of strangers I've met, church-goers who held my hand and wished me peace, children who have passed through our home, older people I felt a familiarity with; all delivered a message to me in a unique way.

The sooner I let go of fear and need for control, the more I learned to trust. When I let go of the "what ifs," I was able to see and experience the joy of the present better. Letting go allowed me to focus on the things that truly mattered at the end of the day. When I gave my time and attention to the beauty of things, I felt the joy within and around me.

Choosing to hand my fate over, learning to trust, and letting it be didn't mean I cared any less or wanted something terrible to happen; I simply accepted that my future was not in my hands, but how I lived today was.

I decided long ago not to give in to fear but to focus my energy on overcoming it instead. I've learned to appreciate the positives that can come from difficult times and see the beauty in uncomfortable times of change and transformation. We forget that difficult paths can lead us to rewarding destinations, beautiful views, and enriching experiences. The task is about much more than control; it's about accepting what we can't fix and choosing to be positive and intentional in the things we can manage. We simply have to let go of things, and when we do, we find more power to focus on the things that we can handle, like our actions and attitudes.

We each go on many rides in our lifetime—some we choose to get on, and others we don't. Some adventures are so exciting that the anticipation is almost as great as the trip itself. Others, we reluctantly hop onto with negative expectations, but get off feeling alive and grateful we decided to go. Some rides scare the shit out of us, and the thought of what lies ahead can paralyze us. The build-up, the waiting, the delays, and detours all create within us a sense of panic and despair.

Yet some of the scariest rides (many of which I didn't voluntarily agree to go on; I boarded kicking and screaming) wound up delivering something that made the worry, fear, and anxiety worth experiencing. It's not always easy to look at things this way, but when you go back to step one; letting go of the things we cannot control and focusing more on the things we can, it's much easier to accept the lesson and enlightenment we might find in a bat-shit, crazy, heart-pounding, gut kicking ride.

If we make it off the ride, we are immediately grateful, and we "touch down" with a newly acquired badge of honor, courage, and sense of conquering. We may not have appreciated every twist, turn, climb and drop of the ride, but we understand what it taught us, how it changed us, what it represented, and how we survived what we doubted we could.

The other important lesson I've learned from these adventurous "rides" we take in our lives is that, often, our expectations of others (or of a specific someone) accompanying us on our ride will lead to disappointment or heartbreak. Some rides, we just have to go on alone. There are no instructions. There's no time for security checks or discussions of evacuation plans, you're just on, and you're going—ready or not.

If you're fortunate, you'll be blessed with loved ones who offer you those reassuring, supportive smiles that encourage you to go on and not back out. Sadly, you'll also find times when you're blindsided by how scared and alone you feel. Don't be surprised when next; you also find yourself feeling angry at those you thought would take this ride with you in the buddy seat without question but didn't.

Sometimes it's meant to be a solo ride, but even single-seaters need someone to meet them at the gate. Throughout your life, the people there to meet you as your feet touch down, you cross the finish line, or you complete the challenge can (and will) change. It will hurt like hell, and it will surprise and disappoint you, but again, focusing on the things you *can* control entails getting off the ride and appreciating those who *are* there for you.

I've been on many rides in my life. Some have been slow and pleasurable, allowing me to savor moments and enjoy seconds. Others have been so fast and unpredictable that my mind could hardly keep up with the racing thoughts. There have been scary and seemingly never-ending ones and heart-pounding, exhilarating, and exciting thrillers.

Every single ride has brought me to the place I am today and made me who I am. Each experience has helped shape who I am, how I feel, and what I believe. Because of these journeys, I have gained a better understanding and ability to relate to others who have been on similar adventures.

Because I've gone on so many rides alone, I believe the greatest gift someone can give to another is being present, even if it's just for reassurance. A comforting figure standing far beneath a ride, holding a hand, washing hair, changing bandages, making a meal, sending an encouraging message, or simply sitting next to someone who is hurting is invaluable. These gestures that show you care make the most significant difference for someone on a ride, and they won't forget.

I think the worst feeling in the world has to be loneliness. Loneliness is the death of hope. It's a dark place no one wants to be, and few will venture to retrieve someone who's stuck there. I know the deep, dark channels of this cave, and my desire to be there for others stems in part from my desperate wish to have someone by my side.

I have endured and experienced a lot. I have lost way too many friends and loved ones, and I find the agony overwhelming at times. Going through life believing that one day my distress would help someone else, I have now realized that I've filled my bag with more relatability than I ever imagined.

But how do all of my experiences and this relatability help me? How has it enriched my life? How does it help me find peace? It begins with accepting that I cannot change people, the past, or circumstances. When I was younger, I wanted to fix everyone else's problems and make things better, and while I still want to do these things, I have learned that it's not my responsibility to solve other peoples' problems for them.

I can start by filling myself up to be a better testament and example to those who want or need it. There is a time and place for everything, and our connections to others are not a coincidence. Those hurting find others who are aching. Those who have been lonely pick up on the neglect of others.

The misunderstood never underestimate the importance of communication and connection. The lost find others who are searching for their way. Those who have known illness live life differently. The abused know what love really is and isn't. The desperate dig deeper and learn to fight harder.

More than just relating to and empathizing with others, living a purposeful life that is personally gratifying is a conscious choice and one that influences and inspires others. It's choosing to rise above circumstances and being willing to serve as a beacon of hope for others who are struggling. It's biting your tongue and choosing your words carefully, knowing that many are listening and remembering them. It's accountability to yourself, your promises, vision, and dreams. It's investing in *you* and realizing that if you don't believe something is possible, you are deciding to fail.

It's not our brokenness but the lack of hope and belief that ruins us. We all experience some form of breaking in our lives, and while it's painful and we are left with scars (visible and invisible), what we do with the pieces are what sets people apart. Our experiences either constrain us or catapult us into action. They either bring us together or pit us against one another. Our behavior can serve to heal or hurt others. We can ignite understanding and compassion, or we can injure and discourage those around us. Those are choices we make.

I have been hurt deeply, I have lost significantly, and I have suffered repeatedly, but I have chosen to believe in a greater purpose, a grander reason, a master plan. I can choose to give into anger and feelings of pain and regret or accept what is and what could be and resist ideas of what *should* be. I have made mistakes in my life, and I'm sure that I have hurt people, even unknowingly. I choose to forgive those who have hurt me, and I hope and pray others will forgive me.

While I didn't immediately see the purpose for my trials, I have been fortunate to find matches to some broken pieces. Had I not been kicked out, I would have never been living on my own in an apartment where I opened the door to a friend in his dark and desperate time. For years, I thought about that night and

SHANE SVOREC

replayed it in my mind. My friend and I reconnected through social media some years ago, but we never discussed that night. It was as if it never happened. I never brought it up out of respect for him, believing he probably wanted to leave it in the past.

When I finally shared my story about my miserable year and a half that I kept secret, he reached out to me, and what he had to say shocked and touched me beyond measure. More than twenty-five years later, a piece of brokenness healed, allowing beautiful light to shine through.

"Once upon a time, a boy lived upstairs from his best friend's girlfriend. The boy was so very troubled and lost. One night he decided that the pain of life was too much. He was drunk and decided to take a bottle of Tylenol and slit his forearm. In his drunken state, he stumbled downstairs to her apartment. To this day, he doesn't know why. Maybe somewhere deep inside, he knew she would care enough to stop him. She saved his life. Cops and the fire department showed up. His stomach was pumped, and his arm sewn up. He hadn't given much thought as to why or what happened. Shame prevented him from reflecting on that night for years, but years later, when sobriety became his life and life was no longer painful, he finally could give thanks to that Angel. Maybe a little remaining shame kept him from thanking her. He just hoped she knew. For the life he had today wouldn't be if it wasn't for her. Shane, you have always been special. My Dad said it, and I knew it too. Mature and kind beyond your years. Reading your experience touched me as I am sure it has touched many who love and respect you. My admiration for you has only grown. We've chewed a bit of the same fat dealing with cancer and knowing how gut-wrenching it is and how truly helpless you feel, especially with regard to children and spouse. I'm proud of you, Shane. As proud as I could be for a friend. And as proud of you as my father would be. I know

it's an ongoing process. . . but I feel your positive mindset and your hope. Most of all. . . I feel your love. I wish nothing but continued healing and strength, my friend. Please keep supplying that lookup girl attitude to this world because we all need it. Sending my love and prayers to you always. And thank you for making that call that saved my life." -Jess

While I had gone through high school carrying invisible burdens that only got heavier as time went on, I now know that being kicked out and living on my own was part of a plan that prepared me for a greater purpose. Had I not lived where I did, when I did, things might have been very, very different.

Growing up so quickly was hard, and though I felt deprived of stability, family to come home to, and many of the same school and social opportunities that my friends had, I was learning that life was not easy. I discovered that I had to work hard and make sacrifices and choices aligned with my priorities to survive. There was no cake and eating it too.

Living for so long in survival mode, I developed a fierce drive and realized that I needed to be my most ardent motivator. I did not have the luxury of having a cheer team to build me up and push or support me. I needed to dig down deep and remember what I was fighting for and what I wanted to achieve. I knew that if I allowed myself to slip into that dark hole of doubt and fear, I would never be able to climb back out, and with no one around, there would be no one to hear me scream or help pull me up.

Having experienced so much in my life has made me who I am. My brokenness has heightened my insight and capacity to understand others' pain and struggles and increased my empathy and compassion. My willingness to be vulnerable has led to the creation of many unexpected connections and meaningful experiences. Through these unpredictable and spontaneous connections, I've found some of the most beautiful moments and priceless memories.

Because of my pain, I see opportunities to share and show love.
Because of my loneliness, I recognize when a friend needs someone.
Because of my silence, I hear unspoken pleas for comfort and care.
Because of my loss, I know greater empathy.
Because of my failings, I understand the gift of forgiveness.
Because of my fear, I focus on hope.
Because of my worry, I put my trust in God and find peace.

The message? We are all broken in our own way, but it doesn't; it shouldn't stop us from believing—believing in more, believing in better, believing in greater! Our broken pieces are not to be hidden but acknowledged, embraced, and repurposed. How we connect these broken pieces is up to us. We can allow them to remain sharp shards of glass that we avoid, or we can appreciate their new, raw shapes and allow them to serve as soft rays of light that soften and inspire others.

Every person in my life helped shape me in some way. I credit strong examples (good and bad) and the influence they had on me. I may have grown up quickly, but my sink or swim upbringing was the best crash course ever. While purpose is not something we immediately see or understand sometimes, we are fortunate to see some of the pieces come together and make purpose out of brokenness.

Another example of this was a message I received recently from a long-time high school friend. It was one of the most refreshing and encouraging messages I've received, as it reminded me of who I am and how much I have stuck to my truth. In her message, she shared a memory she had of me in high school. Reading it now as an adult was the confirmation I needed of my unrelenting conviction to my beliefs, mission, and greater purpose.

Having this glimpse of my sixteen-year-old self reminded me that I have always stood firm in what I believed and refused to give up on my dreams. It reminded me of how far I have come and all I've conquered. While it brought me back to a difficult time, my friend's memory reminded me of that house and all that happened in it. The feelings that I held deep inside, far beneath the strength and courage that others saw, left me wishing I could hug my younger self.

"Shane, I just finished reading your story, and all I can say is that I am not surprised. I have known you since middle school? Maybe? You have ALWAYS wanted to save the world. So much that I think it may have frightened me at times. Maybe it was your compassion and drive to do what you thought would make the world a better place that scared me. It was unfamiliar territory to me then. You are still doing it today by sharing your story - saving the world in your way, sharing your fears, your heartbreak, your pain, and at the same time never forgetting or losing your kindness, your love, your compassion. I remember an argument that you and your dad had when you told him you were going to save the world. You said you didn't know how, but you were going to do your part. You have not changed a bit. We may be a little older now and fighting different battles, but you are still trying to change the world! I agree that there is a positive in everything that happens in our lives. Sometimes it is harder to find, but it is still there. This is probably my favorite thing about you. Good for you for sharing your story and inspiring so many. May GOD bless you and be with you always." Jennifer Johnson Knittel

Although things were not always easy in my relationship with my mom, she taught me to be a strong, independent, and self-reliant woman. She taught me the importance of working hard and never expecting anything. There is no doubt that my love of animals, people, and new experiences all stemmed from my early years, being surrounded by strays of every kind, people of many peculiarities, and wild opportunities to make valuable observations along the way.

For me, I have faith. I know that when I feel alone, I am NOT alone. I know that when I stop struggling and resisting a path or a ride that I have no choice but to travel, I see the things I'm meant to see. It's then that I find beauty and purpose in even the scariest of times. These discoveries prove the sense of wading through my discomfort.

By being there for others and sitting next to them in their times of pain, worry, or fear, I know the deep, unexplainable reward of connecting with another in a difficult time. God's plan may not be my plan, but I have met the people I needed to meet on my many rides. In meeting them, I have experienced peace, healing, hope, encouragement, and forgiveness.

In tough times and in easier times, I know that I have the power within me not just to survive but to live with eyes full of wonder, a spirit full of hope, and a heart full of gratitude. Being an example has always been more important to me than making excuses. I am in the here and now, knowing my presence is filled with purpose, and my tears lead to triumph.

Every minute of silence, every negative thought, every fear that shook me, I chose to resist. Instead, I relied on my faith and focused on the gifts and blessings I had vs. what I lacked. My heart is now overwhelmed with a peaceful stillness that made every frightening minute of silence worthwhile.

I've always known there was purpose in suffering, but now I see it. I respect the gains and personal growth even more after experiencing so many setbacks. I recognize that brokenness allows the light to come in and shine outward for others to see. I've discovered that while I may be broken, I'm still a believer. I believe in goodness, joy, hope, love, and peace, and I believe they are all possible if we choose to look for them, practice them, and share them with others.

This is the story of all the pretty painful pieces along the path to finding purpose.

Play Track 25 (Anyway – Martina McBride) in Broken Little Believer Playlist

<u>Post Participation Survey:</u>

Claim Your Luggage—Take Inventory of Preconceived Notions & Existing Beliefs.

Consider for a moment the questions I asked you at the beginning of this book. Have your responses changed in ***any way***? Has your luggage gotten lighter? Do you feel you can get rid of any of it? Perhaps you've forgotten what you packed and realized that you can leave it behind?

What causes a person to overcome obstacles? What makes a person get up over and over again and keep fighting? From where does one get their will to live? How do people find hope in seemingly hopeless situations? When surrounded by negativity, how does one remain positive? Why do some people choose to forge on while others decide to give up?

Is personal satisfaction determined by how or where a person grows up or the environment in which they lived? Do family dynamics play a part? Is it cultural? Socioeconomics? Is it tied to physical or mental strength or whether someone has strong faith? Does the answer lie in their DNA or psychological makeup? Is it the belief in a higher power, or is it just luck? What do you think? Take a moment and jot down your thoughts now:

_____

_____

_____

_____

_____

_____

_____

_____

_____

_____

_____

_____

_____

_____

_____

_____

_____

_____

_____

Summary of my existing notions and personal beliefs:

I've been asked questions similar to these many times throughout my life. While my responses varied slightly depending on questions and circumstances, part of my response has always remained the same. PEOPLE EXPECTED ME TO FAIL. Not only did people *expect* me to fail, but some even *hoped* I would. By failing, I would prove them right, but by succeeding, I would not only prove them wrong, but more importantly, I would fulfill my vision for my life!

Doubt can become a methodical course to failure, OR it can be a motivating factor. Others' doubt was my GREATEST motivator. When people gave me permission to quit, I couldn't. When they provided endless reasons why I should give up, I searched for a single reason why I shouldn't. When they preyed on my weakness, I honed in on my strength. When they tested my faith, I turned to God. When they sensed my loneliness and tried to take advantage of it, I learned to embrace solitude. When they laughed at me, I used my anger and pain to work harder.

Today, I am an active member of my church, a public servant on both town and school boards, an advocate for children, animals, and the differently-abled. I am a Mental Health First Aid Specialist, Crisis Intervention worker, and founder of The Look Up Girl. Although some cannot imagine growing up the way I did, I am grateful for what I have experienced (both good and bad) as it has given me a greater perspective of people, their varied circumstances, and how I can help.

I have a deep appreciation for all God has given me—especially my husband and children, and for what He has taught me. I grew up quickly and learned to be self-reliant, strong, and motivated to prove people wrong. I am a nurturer by nature, and it is still difficult for me to ask anyone for help.

I struggle to rely on my husband because I learned that when you depend on your spouse, he will cheat or leave you. I have no doubt that it was the miracle of God's Grace that blessed me with a faithful husband who loves me and is a great father and role model to our children. What a fantastic gift it is and something I have always wanted for my children.

My brother also gained greater perspective and clarity from our early life experiences and demonstrates a relentless love and devotion to his two beautiful children. We, no doubt, share a deep-seated conviction to the importance of family and protecting them.

When I look back on my life, I want to know that I made a difference. I want to know that I inspired others, especially my children.

I am thankful for the experiences in my life because I have learned from them how to be a better mother, wife, friend, and child of God, and for that, I am forever grateful, blessed, and loved.

By the Grace of God, I am who I am. *1 Corinthians 15:10*

And on that resounding note, she closed the door
and tried hard not to reopen it.
She created a new song to dance to.
Out of sync and with awkward rhythm,
she knew she had to keep moving.
With every new and uneasy step, she grew.
With every unfamiliar scale of note, she changed.
Her flailing arms and clumsy steps would grow in
confidence and grace after enduring that which was
intended to break her.
What was once so hard, became a symphony of new
beginnings lined by blinding truth and perspective.
The door, tempting to be opened, she nailed shut.
Embracing change, she accepted the lessons, and in
turn, would discover harmony in the beat of her
heart and in the rhythm of her soul.

The Look Up Girl

POSITIVE LIVING

"THE STRENGTH OF A WOMAN IS NOT MEASURED BY HER
ACCOMPLISHMENTS, BUT BY THE OBSTACLES SHE'S
OVERCOME TO ACHIEVE THEM.
THE GRACE OF A WOMAN IS NOT ALWAYS OBSERVED IN
WHAT SHE SAYS, BUT ALSO IN WHAT SHE DOESN'T SAY.
THE HEART OF A WOMAN CAN BE SEEN IN HOW SHE LOVES
AND CARES FOR OTHERS.
HOW DEEPLY SHE LOVES AND CARES, DESPITE HER OWN
PAIN AND SUFFERING, SHOWS THE SIZE OF HER HEART.
THE CHARACTER OF A WOMAN GOES BEYOND WHAT
PEOPLE SEE, BUT MORE IMPORTANTLY, WHAT SHE DOES
WHEN NO ONE IS WATCHING.
THE DETERMINATION OF A WOMAN IS NOT IN THE CHANCES
SHE TAKES, BUT THE SACRIFICES SHE WILLING TO MAKE.
THE RESILIENCY OF A WOMAN IS SEEN,
NOT JUST IN HER ABILITY TO SURVIVE A FALL, BUT IN HER
WILL TO GET BACK UP AGAIN." ©
Shane Svorec

The Look Up Girl 《

POSITIVE LIVING

Endnotes

1. Rick Warren, "A Quote from The Purpose Driven Life," Goodreads, *Rick Warren Quotable Quotes,* April 28, 2021, https://www.goodreads.com/quotes/127251-other-peopl e-are-going-to-find-healing-in-your-wounds.

2. Peter, Paul, and Mary. "Wedding Song" (There Is Love), 25th Anniversary Concert, June 17th, 2013, https://www. youtube.com/watch?v=RrTfNTzAvYY.

3. Heaven's Magic. "Watch Out for 666," SOS:20 Minutes to Go, Aurora Productions, 1990, https://www.youtube. com/watch?v=jmHNnCDvKf4.

4. James Taylor. "Fire and Rain," Sweet Baby James, BBC in Concert, November 16, 1970, https://www.youtube.com/ watch?v=_1nKGVDhQ60.

5. Miranda Lambert. "The House That Built Me," March 31, 2010, https://www.youtube.com/watch?v=DQYNM6 SjD_o.

About the Author

Shane Svorec is a lifelong writer and author who currently resides in New Jersey, along with her husband, three children, rescue dogs, and chickens.

Best described as a traveling gypsy with the heart of a hippie and the faith of a missionary, Shane uses her hardships and tragedies to inspire and encourage others. Refusing to allow her past or circumstances to define her, she searches for the light in dark times and shows others how they can do the same.

Having traveled across the country as a child, she's lived in more places than she can count and has stories to connect them all like destination dots on a map. Shane writes with such colorful and palpable descriptions; readers feel they can see the world through the backseat of a VW bus along with her.

She credits her challenging and unconventional upbringing for becoming an observant, resilient, adventurous, flexible, brave, and empathetic woman and honest writer.

Once a child of the state, who later became a foster parent, Shane has made it her life's mission to advocate for those without a voice. A proud mother, animal lover, believer in angels, and faith-filled woman, she is highly involved in her community, an active member of her church, public servant, member of her local Board of Education, mental health and crisis intervention worker, and perpetual peacemaker and kindness spreader.

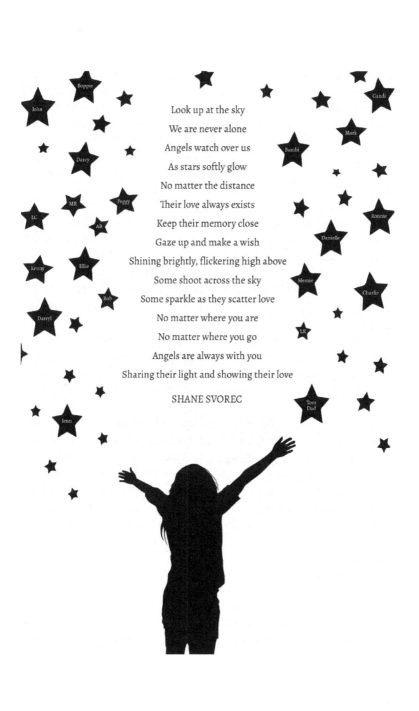

Look up at the sky
We are never alone
Angels watch over us
As stars softly glow
No matter the distance
Their love always exists
Keep their memory close
Gaze up and make a wish
Shining brightly, flickering high above
Some shoot across the sky
Some sparkle as they scatter love
No matter where you are
No matter where you go
Angels are always with you
Sharing their light and showing their love

SHANE SVOREC

The journey doesn't have to end here!

Continue the adventure
Connect with Shane Svorec

Author
Motivational Speaker
Positive Influencer
Event Writer
Creative Marketer
Wellness Advocate
Mental Health Spokesperson
Peace Builder

www.ShaneSvorec.com

CPSIA information can be obtained
at www.ICGtesting.com
Printed in the USA
BVHW042117200621
610103BV00008B/119

9 781647 468071